WHY BE LONELY?

Why be LONELY?

Edward E. Ford
&
Robert L. Zorn

ARGUS COMMUNICATIONS Niles, Illinois

FIRST EDITION

Printed in the United States of America

ARGUS COMMUNICATIONS
7440 Natchez Avenue
Niles, Illinois 60648

International Standard Book Number: 0-913592-50-1
Library of Congress Number 75-29884

1 2 3 4 5 6 7 8 9 0

TO WILLIAM GLASSER, M.D.

Contents

Preface

Everyone would undoubtedly agree that we have made great advances since the time of the cave man. Many people look at today's great cities, airlines, freeways, and shopping malls and conclude that man has come a long way.

But in spite of these achievements, many men and women live a lonely and isolated existence. People say they have lived in a community for years and do not even know their neighbors. They go to work, drive around, eat out, watch TV, see a show, go to parties, and yet say their lives are empty and unfulfilled. They say they are bored. Depression and loneliness are rapidly becoming major concerns of modern life.

Although man has been able to master much of his environment, he has not yet learned to fully enjoy life or build lasting relationships. In the past few years problems with interpersonal relationships seem to be worse than ever, as evidenced by a rapidly increasing divorce rate and court dockets filled with personal lawsuits.

Part of the problem is directly related to the time people spend in front of their television sets or at the movies. The skills of human interaction must be developed and continually improved. Merely observing human interaction on a screen is no substitute for getting to know each other and sharing ourselves with others. Learning to love and to relate successfully to others is what life is all about.

The high degree of mobility in our society, where one out of every five families changes residence every year, has reduced the traditional family ties and neighborhood friendships to a minimum. It has created a vacuum for many whose lives were once filled with love and friends.

Thus with modern affluence, mobility, and television comes a new form of loneliness—that of being agonizingly bored and lonely while surrounded by others. Never before have *so many* experienced this kind of painful loneliness. Life is the only ball game there is, yet so many sit it out as observers in the grandstand.

The lonely believe no one cares about them. They feel worthless. They despair of ever making and maintaining a warm, authentic human relationship. They fear involvement. They avoid risk. However, there is always hope. If a person is willing to work at getting involved, he can succeed. Involvement and a meaningful life *are possible.*

This book, like our first book, *Why Marriage?,* is an attempt to popularize and explain "reality therapy." We have dedicated it to Dr. William Glasser, president and founder of the Institute for Reality Therapy in Los Angeles, California, a man who has truly demonstrated a way to help others. Dr. Glasser is the author of *Reality Therapy, Schools Without Failure,* and *The Identity Society.* He is a man whose own clear thinking has cut through the maze of theories and therapies to offer new hope to the lonely, the frustrated, and those who feel the pain of failure.

We would also like to acknowledge the profound influence our wives have had on our lives. To Hester Ford and Joan Zorn go a great deal of love and appreciation.

Finally we thank Joy Gaetano who made valuable comments and suggestions and typed the many revisions of this book.

Youngstown, Ohio
June 26, 1975 Edward E. Ford and Robert L. Zorn

What is reality therapy?

Reality therapy recognizes that the basic need of people is to attain a success identity from which comes the strength to live responsibly and to handle the problems and stresses of life. The pathway to a success identity, or good self-image, is through developing the ability to make and maintain genuine human relationships and through seeing oneself as a worthwhile person, both in one's own eyes and in the eyes of others. We receive our worth and dignity as human beings from what we do in life.

It assumes that we all have the same need for a success identity and internal strength but that we vary in our ability to fulfill this need; that to be worthwhile we must maintain a satisfactory standard of behavior; that responsible individuals fulfill their needs in a way that neither infringes on the rights of others nor deprives others of the ability to fulfill their needs.

Reality therapy is a method of working with people through caring, from which comes the initial strength a person needs to change. It states that a person is responsible for his own behavior—not society, not the environment, not heredity, not the past, but each person, now. Reality therapy urges individuals to gain the strength to change through involvement with others. It is through human relationships, honest interest in others, that lonely people who believe they have no one and are of no value can gain the strength to find self-respect and self-confidence.

Reality therapy states that people who fail in life do so because they have made poor choices of behavior due to an inability and lack of strength to become involved in authentic human relationships. They must first be taught to evaluate what they are doing and then how to plan a better way of living their life. It is only through changing their behavior that they will begin to feel better and gain a sense of self-worth.

Reality therapy is not a textbook or magic solution to problems. It is accepting responsibility for what one does. It is not looking for blame or finding fault or dwelling on the past or feeling sorry for oneself. It is accepting life as it is now and striving to do better by changing one's behavior. It is life. It is action. It is hard work. It is the way you live with yourself and with others.

Chapter one

What's happening to us?

Run. Run. Try to find yourself. Hurry or you'll miss yourself. I'm trying to find myself. I'm trying to find others. Who am I? I'm bored. I'm depressed. I'm so lonely.

I look at people around me. They are different, yet the same. I see people laughing at parties, going to work, talking to others. But many are lonely. Their life is empty. They are looking for something to fill the void.

From Maine to Florida, from the East Coast to the West Coast, people are searching. They move from one city to another, from one neighborhood to another, join clubs, pop a pill, go shopping in crowded stores, take a drink, but still the pain is there—loneliness is there.

What causes depression? Boredom? Loneliness? Anxiety? Why all the present misery and emptiness? Whatever happened to living in a neighborhood where you knew everybody, had lots of close friends, and shared good times?

But don't worry; all our troubles are going to end. Happiness is just around the corner. Our problems can be quickly solved. A new day is dawning in a new land because the fantasy world of TV is here. Are you wet under the arms? There is an underarm spray that lasts twice as long. Have a migraine headache? Then get quick relief from fast-acting aspirin. Whatever it is, "We've got the product that's made for what you've got." "We've got the real thing." It can be instant, freeze-dried or perked, but it's magic. It will turn you on.

Has the world really changed? Are we actually living in different times? Are people today really apathetic and indifferent to the needs of others? Have our values changed that much? What is causing the spiraling increase in divorces? In suicides?

Much attention has been given to these questions. It is evident that our times are different and people have changed. Our basic needs have stayed the same, but our priorities have changed. We attempt to fulfill age-old needs in new ways.

What has caused these changes? What is bringing about the increase in loneliness in our society?

I think there are three prime causes. First, boredom. We have a great deal of free time, and we have not learned how to use it. Second, many people do not know how to make and maintain good friendships. Third, our expectations are higher than ever before.

People have always looked for self-worth through achievement, first looking at how they were doing and then comparing themselves with others and how they were doing. You might say life was based on comparisons. If we saw our own life as being better off than another's, then our own self-worth was greatly enhanced. We immediately felt better. In fact, the better we looked on our scale of comparisons, the better we felt. If we had the *best* car, the *biggest* house, the *most* money, the *highest* position—we were on top. A person used to feel like a success because he could see he was better off than a lot of other people. This was the process used by many people for years to fulfill their basic needs of worth and value.

But times are different. Things have changed. We still compare ourselves to others, but the feedback we receive (even if it is good feedback) does not sustain happiness or make us feel good very long. Happiness seems to be more illusive than ever. Let's first take a look at the difficulty people have in avoiding boredom.

People search constantly for things which are fun and make them feel good. There is so much to do we are swamped with choices. It is like being in a big candy store and trying to decide which piece of candy to eat first.

Many people undoubtedly look for immediate fun and pleasure, and there is nothing wrong with that. It is just that since immediate pleasure is not very enduring, people have to continue to search for more pleasure and more things to do.

No one wants a life of drudgery and boredom. No one wants to be lonely and depressed. But the secret of feeling good for a long period of time is in the *kind* of pleasure being sought. It is the difference between fleeting and lasting happiness. Everyone has snatches of happiness, but some cannot hold on to these moments as long as they would like to.

Instant, sensuous pleasure is not as rewarding or lasting as the long-range pleasure we derive from the more meaningful things we do. Let's say you like music. Listening to records is fun. But if you want lasting happiness and good feelings from your music, you have to do more—like getting involved in playing an instrument, or taking voice lessons and joining a band or choir. You attend concerts and enjoy a sense of involvement with others who like music. This kind of pleasure will lead you toward more lasting good feelings and a sense of self-worth.

Perhaps the outline on the following page will help to show the differences between the two kinds of pleasure.

Immediate Pleasure

Long-range Enjoyment

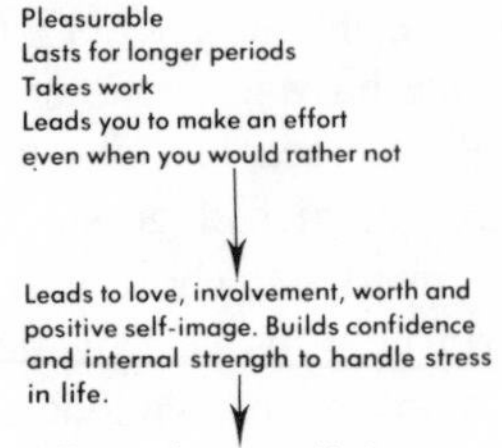

No criticism is intended of short-term enjoyment; it is simply a matter of knowing what to do to get a little more out of life. If you want lasting good feelings, you have to do different things than if you want to feel good just for a moment.

That is why people who are lonely or depressed are often told by a friend, a spouse, or a counselor that they should do something active, perhaps start a hobby. Hobbies require effort and fulfill the requirements of long-range enjoyment. You pick a hobby because you like it and it has meaning to you. You are interested in it and you spend hours at hobbies such as gardening, refinishing furniture, ceramics, leather tooling, or maybe rock collecting. People find these activities enjoyable because they find a more lasting sense of happiness and self-fulfillment from them.

Hobbies, like other long-range pleasure pursuits, offer the possibility of involvement with other people, and that is good. There are clubs for almost all hobbies, and these clubs offer pleasant conversation and involvement with people who share a common interest. We also receive a lasting sense of pride and accomplishment as we grow proficient in our hobbies.

Exaggerated expectations are another cause of increased loneliness. We have come to expect more out of life. Part of this is due to the fantasy world of TV; part of it is due to all the assurances of big government that the general welfare of everyone is assured; part of it is the attitude taken by each succeeding generation—its children should be better off than their parents. With all these factors converging, it is very easy to expect more from life than life has to offer.

There is nothing wrong in high goals if you are willing to work to see that these goals become a reality. The problem occurs when the reality does not equal one's expectations. If the reality of your life is better than you expect, you feel good. But if it is less than you expect, the result is unhappiness and bad feelings. It is important to set realistic expectations and to look at the practical realities of life. That is not to say you do not dream and aim high. You can aim for the moon, as long as you are aware of your abilities and talents and of life's possibilities.

Today's commercials and advertisements tell us that if we use a certain type of deodorant, toothpaste, shampoo, or soap we will be happier, sexier, healthier, and more popular. If this were true, fights, arguments, and divorce courts would all have disappeared. But it is just the opposite. For instance, in the county in which I live, the number of divorces granted actually outnumbered the marriages last year. The media, especially TV, has increased our expectations of love, and thus we are less willing to tolerate the realities of an authentic human relationship.

Whether a person is married, single, or living with another, the feeling of rejection, of *not* being wanted, is one of the most devastating things that can ever happen to that person. It never feels good to feel lonely or to have no one with whom you can talk things over and share some of your life's experiences.

If everyone needs love and affection, why don't we work harder to fulfill this need? Because for some people, the harder they work at getting along, the further love seems from their grasp. The answer then is not just hard work; it is knowing *how and what to do*.

I recently called in a radio repairman to fix a stereo set. He came out, fiddled with a few wires, and the set worked beautifully.

"What's the charge?" I asked.

"Twenty-five dollars," he replied.

"Twenty-five dollars? For what? All you did was fiddle with a few wires. You didn't even check a tube."

"Well," the repairman said slowly, "ten dollars is the service charge for coming out. And fifteen dollars is for knowing what to do."

I thought about it for a minute. The fifteen dollars, in essence, was for his ability to make the set work again.

So it is in life. I could have fiddled with all the wires in the stereo, too, but I probably would never have made it work. So it is not just work that makes a relationship go or makes your life a happy one. *It is knowing the right thing to do at the right place and the right time. It is knowing how and what to do.*

It is important to remember that everyone experiences some sadness and depression. The secret is in knowing how to get rid of these unwanted feelings as quickly as possible. The idea is to bounce back and be happy and involved with friends once more.

Nobody ever became a success all by himself. It takes help. Lots of help. The more successful we are, the more people have helped us along the way.

Successful people will tell you they have many friends who helped them at various stages of their careers. Early in life, they had people who believed in them, encouraged them, and never gave up on them. They had close friends and relatives who had faith in them. Ultimately, they gained the internal strength and determination to succeed at whatever they set their mind to do.

Others have not developed this internal confidence and strength. They need help from someone who cares about them and who will not give up on them. They need to gain confidence in themselves and to experience some success. They need to know how to work at finding a better way of life.

Regardless of where you are in your own life, I hope this book will help you in your personal development.

Chapter two

How we function

Everyone who is lonely tries to overcome the empty, depressing feelings found in loneliness, but many aren't able to do this. They continue to feel alienated and helpless. They seem to be locked in on failure, on misery, on themselves. Their bad feelings make it difficult for them to change their way of life.

Feelings have a two-fold purpose. The first purpose is to keep us constantly aware of *how* we are doing, both physically and psychologically. Feelings tell us when we need food, how we are getting along with others, and if what we are doing gives us any value as persons.

The second purpose of feelings is to help build the internal strength we need in order to handle the stress and problems of life. This is done by good feelings, which constantly increase our self-confidence and faith in ourselves, and thereby provide us with internal strength.

In order to understand how all this happens, let's look at how we function. The process is not difficult to understand or complicated. We all have a brain, a nervous system, and feelings. The brain figures out what to do, the nervous system evaluates how we are doing, and our feelings are the signals telling us how we're doing. Figure 1 shows a diagram of this process.

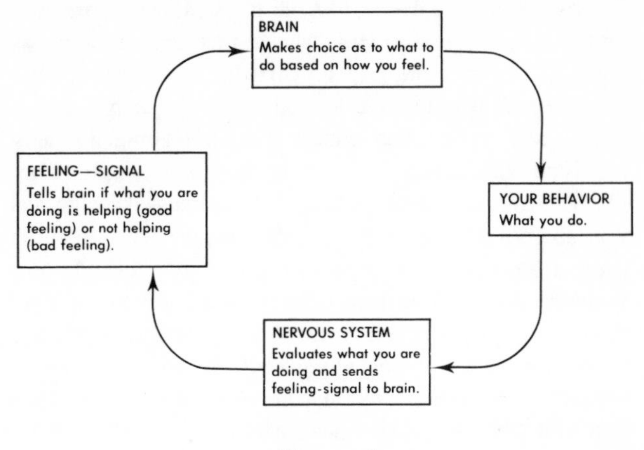

Figure 1

Suppose a man needs water. The nervous system would automatically send a signal to his brain telling him he needs water. If we were to ask him how he felt, he would say, "I'm thirsty." This feeling of thirst is, for the moment, how the person feels. His brain could decide to ignore this signal, and he would continue to feel thirsty. If he does drink a glass of water, the signal he would then receive is a feeling of pleasure which comes from the reduction (or elimination) of thirst. He has satisfied a basic need. Once thirst has gone, the brain could turn its attention elsewhere.

The important point to remember here is that, when we experience these physical needs, *we know what to do instinctively*. We don't have to teach children what thirst or hunger require. They know what to do. Like animals, humans have certain instinctive reactions.

Our physical needs like food, water, shelter, and rest are easy to determine. And whenever we do something and it feels good, we know that what we are doing is working.

Our psychological needs, like our physical needs, are built into us neurologically. However, our psychological needs are much more complex and difficult to determine. For instance, all people have a need for other people. Loneliness is a feeling that comes from not being humanly involved with others. It comes to those who would rather observe life than participate in it. Loneliness is a sign that you are not meeting basic psychological needs. Ignoring these signs is a tragic mistake because they tell you how you are doing. You receive signals all the time. Your system is always functioning. When you feel good, you know your life is going along well. When you feel bad, something is wrong. When your brain receives a signal that you feel lonely, you need people.

Although we can fool ourselves into thinking many things, *what is always real is how we feel*. Try as you may, you can never convince yourself you feel differently from the way you really feel. It is hard to understand people who say they are trying to discover their "real" feelings. At any given time, you feel either good or bad. Whether you feel depressed or lonely or upset does not really matter. What matters is that when you feel bad, something is wrong.

Feelings have been built into us for a reason. They keep us informed about how we are doing. Without feeling, we would all be in trouble. When we feel good, what we are doing is helping us. When we feel lousy, what we are doing obviously is not helping us.

It is easy to continue to do things which give us good feelings. What is difficult is figuring out what to do when we feel pain. What we should do is look around to see what we can do differently.

I define psychological needs as those needs we all have for love and worth; in other words, the need for people and the need to have value as a person, needs satisfied by what we do.

When we feel good in relation to our psychological needs, we know what to do. We take a look at *what we are doing* and continue the same actions. If I enjoy golfing with someone, I schedule another game with him. Thus to feel good around people, I look at *what I do when I am with others and feeling good,* and I do the same things again.

The problem is how to handle the bad feelings which come from unsuccessful attempts to be humanly involved with others. There are six reasons why it is difficult to overcome these feelings.

First, bad feelings do not tell us what to do to feel good again. Unlike physical needs, which are instinctive, the bad feelings which come from our inability to make authentic human relationships do not tell us what to do. The lonely, depressed, and miserable alcoholic knows something is wrong. But he does not know what to do to feel good again.

There are bad feelings in the physiological realm which are very precise, like the pain from a stone in your shoe. You can tell exactly where it hurts and what to do about it. Psychological pain is something altogether different. It is vague, and you ache all over. You feel upset. Depression, anxiety, boredom, loneliness—these feelings do not tell us precisely what to do or what is wrong.

Second, the pain of the bad feelings tend to overwhelm the brain, making it hard for us to figure out what to do. No one has ever come to me for counseling because of physical needs. No one has ever said, "I'm thirsty; I don't know what to do," or "I've been cold lately, and I'm not sure what to do about it." People come to see me because they have not been able to figure out what to do to meet their psychological and social needs.

To a person who has not suffered the hopeless, painful feeling of loneliness or depression, this may be difficult to understand. When you feel good, it is easy to think about solutions to problems and to plan ahead. But when you are hurting and feeling bad, it is difficult to think. The bad feelings tend to overwhelm the brain.

What happens is that the pain of the bad feelings not only makes it hard to think about what to do but overwhelms the brain to a point where *the painful feeling begins to guide the behavior of the person* (see Figure 2).

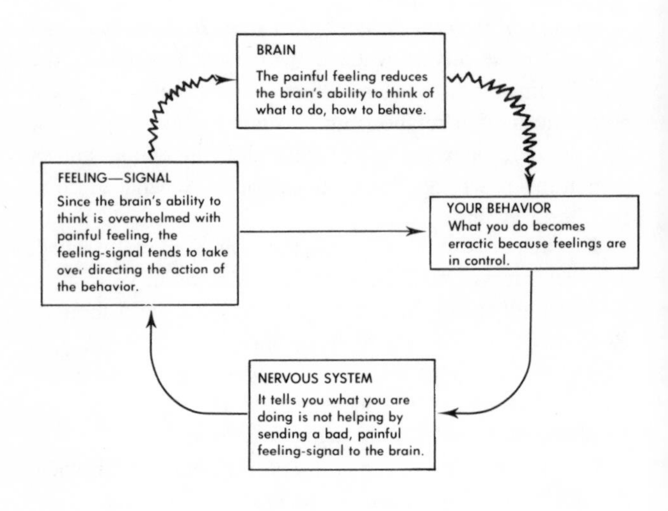

Figure 2

A person who is angry, for example, often lets his feelings guide his behavior. Because feelings are generally erratic, his behavior becomes erratic and he may strike out at another. When his feelings of anger subside and his brain is back in control, he realizes his action has not helped the relationship.

A person in such a case will generally reflect and brood on what he has done and feel worse. He feels bad about feeling bad. What he should do is look at what he can do *in the present* to change things for the better. Ultimately that is where a real change in behavior can occur, eventually leading to better feelings.

Bad feelings turn people inward. They find it harder and harder to think clearly because their feelings, which have taken over directing their behavior, are as painful as ever. They begin functioning on a different level, the feeling level instead of the thoughtful, cerebral level. This is the reason for wild behavior when we feel extremely upset or unhappy. The seat of responsibility, how we think, the value judgments and decisions we make—all these are centered in the brain, not in feelings. Since feelings are highly erratic and fluctuating, behavior controlled by feelings becomes irresponsibly erratic, and ultimately it gets out of control.

Third, in order to overcome bad feelings we have to learn what to do. Learning how to make and build lasting relationships is a continual process.

Unlike the need for water, food, or rest, which is known instinctively, the need to be humanly involved must be learned by experience—from someone who cares. For a child to learn to care, he must experience someone caring for him and loving him. Caring cannot be taught by talking about love or reading love stories. It must be experienced.

Listening is taught by someone who asks thoughtful questions and listens noncritically to answers. When someone who cares listens respectfully, the child learns to listen. We teach what we model. The old saying, "Actions speak louder than words," is all too true.

Fourth, bad feelings make a person harder to get along with. It is hard to be warm to a lonely or depressed person. His misery tends to alienate others. It is like being around someone who has rude manners or an annoying laugh. We tend to back away.

Also, a lonely person often finds it uncomfortable to be around happy people. It seems to make his own misery worse. For instance, a person who bowls Two-hundred consistently would tend to make a beginner feel inadequate. So it is with a person in misery. He does not want to be around other people, especially if they are happy or successful. That only makes him feel worse. As his thoughts center more and more on himself and on how bad he feels, he tends to immobilize himself. The more immobilized he becomes, the harder it is for him to move toward others. The result is severe loneliness and depression, and a feeling of hopelessness.

To escape his misery, the person behaves in even more erratic ways. I hear clients say: "I don't know why I do these things." "Why did I yell?" "What's happening to me?" "I don't know what came over me."

We have all seen examples of this kind of behavior at one time or another. It is usually followed by excuses such as: "I couldn't help it." "I just did it." "I'm sorry, but something takes hold of me." "I can't help myself."

Fifth, bad feelings tend to cause us to think of how bad we feel and in that way make us feel worse. Sometimes counselors talk about bad feelings. Ultimately, I believe this makes a person feel worse. All that thinking about our depression does is to increase awarenesss and the pain of the feeling. If you go to a funeral home to offer your sympathy to a friend, you would not discuss how he feels. Or if you had a toothache, and the dentist wanted to discuss the pain and how much it hurt, you would probably think he was acting a little crazy. Tooth repair is what is needed.

Yet with those who feel lonely and depressed, the natural tendency is for them to think about how bad they feel, thus making themselves suffer more than ever.

Sixth, the painful feelings of failure and loneliness tend to drain the internal strength necessary to handle stress. The misery of depression and loneliness reduces continually the strength needed to change the situation. The longer a person suffers, the more difficult it is to change. This is because what little strength he had continues to diminish. Failure begets failure.

Bad feelings also reduce faith and self-confidence. Many couples who come in for marriage counseling have lost faith in their marriage. The job of the counselor is to rebuild strength and confidence so the couple can handle the stress and problems of married life. Many individuals have the same difficulty in building confidence, especially the aged and those serving long-term prison sentences. Their hope for a better future is gone. What little strength they might have had has been drained by long hours of lonely depression.

A person in the throes of painful feelings knows he is in trouble. If his problems persist and he continues to feel badly, his life looks like the diagram in Figure 3.

The funny thing about feelings is that we feel either good or bad at any given moment in our life. If you were to hit your thumb with a hammer and be handed $1,000 at the same time, maybe that would be one of those rare occasions when you felt both good and bad at the same time; but usually people feel one way or the other.

When a person feels lonely or depressed, it is his inability to figure out what is wrong and what to do about it that causes him harm. Saying, "I feel lousy," is a signal that

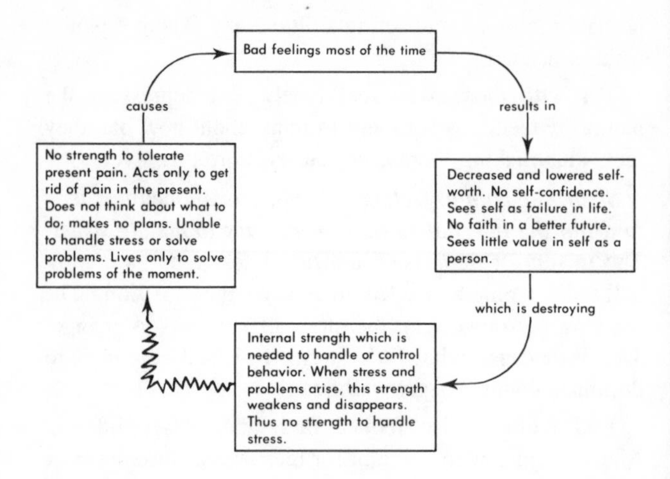

Figure 3

positive action is being called for. He has not learned from past experience what to do to feel better when he becomes depressed. If he did learn it at one time and is now in difficulty, then he has forgotten what to do, is not actively working at changing his life, or lacks the strength to do so.

For instance, a person who was once very active, who did things such as swimming, playing tennis, and leading a busy social life, will become bored and lonely if he isolates himself from others and stops being active. If you ask him, "When did your troubles start?" or "When did you begin to feel bad?" he will tell you his worries became acute about the same time he stopped being so active. However, he probably never associated his negative feelings with what he had stopped doing.

That is always the problem with bad feelings; they tell us that what we are doing is not good, but they do not tell us what to do. The mind concentrates primarily on what to do, which only serves to make us do it even more. Saying "don't smile" always causes a smile; "don't eat that cake'' generally causes us to eat the cake; ''don't feel lonely'' ends up making us feel more lonely; and ''don't argue'' causes more arguments. The mind concentrates on the positive, and the word ''don't'' does not register.

Negative feelings also tend to immobilize our creative thought processes, whereas good feelings encourage us to think more freely. Good feelings bring more good feelings, and bad feelings bring more bad feelings—unless we break the cycle by figuring out what we should do to get back in the swing of things.

The reason bad feelings are hard to cope with is because of the pain we receive from them. There is no pain involved with good feelings. That is why we easily know what to do when we feel good. A person who is living his life effectively functions in the way indicated in Figure 4.

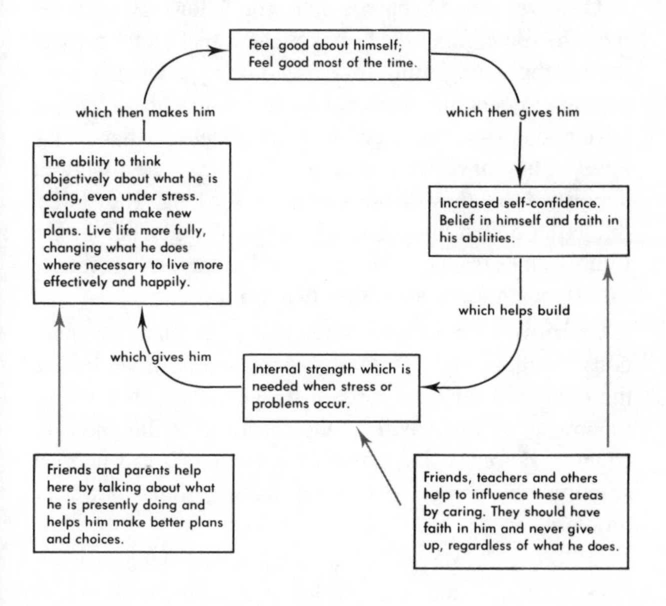

Figure 4

As this wheel of success begins to move, each segment influences the next. Just as a snowball rolling down a hill will get bigger and bigger, the successful person's life seems to get better and better. People might say, "He gets all the breaks." And to some, it may seem like he does; but then that is the difference between one who tries to make something out of life and one who does not. The successful person possesses the internal strength to build success out of failure, to turn defeat into victory.

At times of stress, when bad feelings do occur, strong and successful people have enough momentum to continue their forward progress. They are driven by hope and confidence. Weak and unsuccessful people are not. A minor problem to a weak person easily becomes a major hurdle. They make mountains out of mole hills.

Observe some happy people you know. Even when they do something which makes them feel bad—perhaps saying the wrong thing to a friend or experiencing some personal rejection or flunking an exam—these people have enough internal strength and confidence to handle the upset. They have what it takes. They may get lonely or depressed, but they do not stay down for long. They fail at things, too, but they bounce back. Their belief in the future comes from overcoming past failures and in essence experiencing more successes than failures.

Often we hear the expression that a person has tremendous "willpower." This can be understood if we realize there are two separate parts of willpower which combine to appear as one. *Will* is the desire or willingness to change. *Power* is the degree of commitment and internal strength one brings to bear in solving some particular problem.

Willpower is developed initially as you believe others care about you and you develop your own ability to care about others. This takes time to build. An alcoholic, for example, begins to want to change because of the friendship he receives from others who care about him. The strength he needs comes at first from those who care about him and support him in a relational way as he goes through the long process of rehabilitation. Later, as he grows more confident, he begins to rely on his own strength which has been developing. As he begins to help others, he gains even more strength.

People who can change quickly and get right on with leading a more effective, happy life have some internal strength to begin with. Many who come to see me have this basic strength and only need a little help. You learn to handle stress little by little. As you gain more strength and confidence, you can handle more stress. It is not like jumping into a swimming pool with one big splash and getting wet all at once. You are better off in handling stress to wade into it gradually, taking only as much as you can manage at one time.

A young couple I counseled recently had been separated for several months. They began building depth and strength back into their relationship by doing active, enjoyable things together several hours every Saturday evening. After a few weeks, they tried seeing each other three nights a week. A month of that and they decided to move back together. All went well for a few days until the same old stressful situation occurred—she came home late from work.

This had been a source of agitation before. They both worked, but Tom had a job where the hours were regular. He quit everyday at five o'clock sharp. Dorothy often had to work overtime at the data processing company. How to handle this stress successfully was important if they were to stay married and enjoy their relationship.

We started with small steps. We looked for alternatives to this problem as well as for things they could continue to do that they found enjoyable. They had a sailboat and decided to spend more time sailing together. As for the problem, we came up with numerous solutions: she could call if she were going to be late; she could ask her boss if she could reduce or eliminate working overtime; she could look for another job; she could tell Tom in advance when she thought she might be late; she could call Tom at work; and so on. Tom could get a snack, and they could eat later when she got home; he could make the dinner for them on the evenings she was late; he could meet her at work and they could go out to eat.

Once they started attacking the problem instead of each other, they could once again enjoy a close, rewarding relationship. By the way, Tom and Dorothy solved their problem by combining several of these alternatives. A single solution did not work; it took several. But they took on the future one week at a time. Real strength comes when a person decides upon a course of action, accepts the responsibility for what he does, follows through, and finds success.

Another aspect of behavior is the so-called need to ventilate feelings. Although it has become popular recently, to vent feelings is not the best way to change your life. Teaching people to ventilate feelings only shows them how to let off steam. It doesn't solve anything. The problems don't go away. If you feel hungry, does yelling about your problem put food in your stomach? Hunger is a feeling resolved by food. Crimes of passion, like certain murders, are the ultimate in allowing feelings rather than reason to tell you what to do.

Somehow, the beneficial effects of getting others to talk about how they feel (without connecting their feelings to what they are doing) or encouraging others to react to how they feel have always been a mystery to me. These methods seem to imply that bad feelings are some sort of mysterious force or sickness that has possessed the body and is something over which we have no control.

And furthermore, talking about or reacting to feelings implies that somehow things will get better (the bad feelings will go away). If someone who is warm and kind talks with a person, it is bound to feel better if previously they had no one to talk to—regardless of *what* they talk about. But the good feeling will only be temporary unless they begin to change what they are doing.

Thus many persons believe that feelings should be dealt with as entities in themselves. Yet this seems like treating the symptom, not the cause, of the problem. Drugs are a good example. Feel depressed, take a drug. Feel nervous, take a pill. All you learn from drugs is that your problems seem to be momentarily solved. But drugs are not therapeutic, and by themselves do not build the internal strength needed to handle life's problems. If medication calms a person and eventually allows someone to help him evaluate his present actions, it is helpful.

You feel better over a longer period of time from acting responsibly and changing what you are actually doing, not just from taking medicine. Drugs may be necessary for some for a short time, but constant reliance on them teaches ineffective ways of living and does not solve problems. For instance, you lose your temper because your migraines are back and you forgot to take your pill. You should be looking at better ways of handling your anger. Ignoring our brain—that is, our ability to think—is to ignore our greatest asset. Dulling the brain or rendering it ineffective with a large dose of drugs is even worse.

Bad feelings tell us things, if we stop and analyze the message. They tell us: that what we are doing is not helping us; to stop what we are doing; and to start doing something else. Bad feelings should be signals which tell us to think out and reevaluate what we are doing. In order to do this, we have to use our brain. We have to ask ourselves: What have we done in the past which we enjoyed? What has given us feelings of self-worth? What is relevant to us? Who are the people we enjoy being with? The answers to these questions are what make us feel good.

A recently divorced woman moved to a town in northern New England. She had sufficient income from her former husband, a job, and her children were away at college. To keep from being lonely, she invited a neighbor over for dinner at least once a week. She joined a health club and sewed as a volunteer for a crippled children's hospital.

She realized she had to do certain things to keep herself alert and happy. She did not know anybody. She was a stranger in town, but she had the sense and courage to figure out what to do. It worked for her. She used her internal strength and confidence and worked at making new friends. She met many people in that little New England town and soon became involved. She did not just feel sorry for herself. She looked at what she could do, and in the doing she felt better.

You constantly evaluate yourself as you go through life. When you do certain things and people tell you, "That's a good job," you gain in your sense of self-worth. If you also have developed good relationships with people, then these two behaviors (one that gets you love and another that gets you worth) will help you to become strong. You will build a success identity and a positive self-image. You will develop the inner self-concept that tells you, "I am a person who is strong," and "I can do it."

Chapter three

Changing the way we live

Today we have many gadgets and machines that do a lot of work for us. Of course, they are convenient and tremendous worksavers, but they often lead people to believe in easy solutions. TV has weekly miracles where crimes and murders are solved in sixty minutes or less. This also leads many people to believe there are easy solutions to problems they face in real life. However, in reality there are no easy solutions to many problems. Some problems just take time, hard work and lots of perseverance. That is what it takes to change the way you live, to change your habits.

First, you must have the desire or motivation to change and to try something new. If you are stuck in a rut, things will not get better by themselves. Everyone has ups and downs. The difference between those who are occasionally down or unhappy and those who are almost always severely depressed for long periods of time is that those who are seldom upset know what to do to find happiness again. They have the internal strength and confidence to do something when they feel low and depressed. How do they do it? How do some people have the ability to bounce back and live their lives effectively while others continue to live in misery?

Thoreau once said, "The mass of men lead lives of quiet desperation." The fact is, they do not have to. Your life can be pleasant and enjoyable—if you choose it to be so and work at making it so. Abraham Lincoln said, "Most folks are about as happy as they make up their minds to be." Maybe it would be helpful to visualize the ups and downs in a person's life on a happiness scale as in Figure 5.

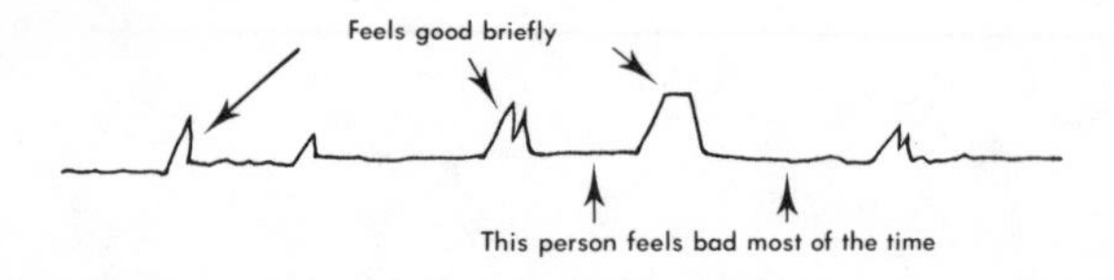

Figure 5

Notice how long the gloomy periods are and how fleeting the good moments are in this type of life. It is not a very enjoyable life, and yet many live that way. The basic pattern of ups and downs in their lives stay about the same from one year to the next. Things never seem to get any better. They do not seem to get any worse either; it is just that people with this life-style always seem to be unhappy.

Other people seem to be accomplishing more and more and to be enjoying themselves. They have a happy attitude. What makes the difference? Let's take a look at another life pattern shown in Figure 6. Here we see a person who enjoys his life most of the time, and thus the ups last longer than the downs, are less frequent and less painful.

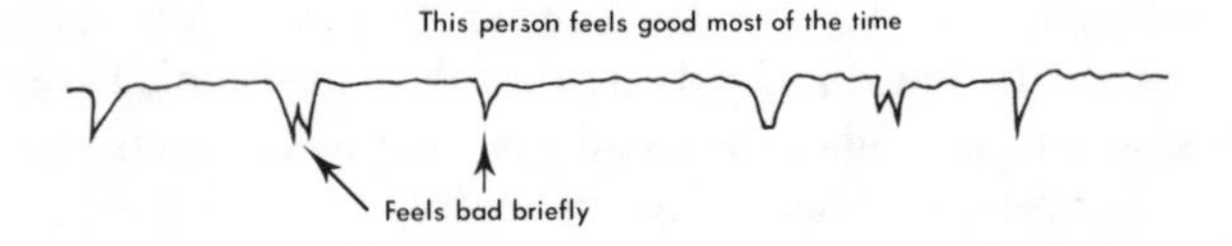

Figure 6

The problem with those who lead lives of continual misery and loneliness is they have no self-confidence. They see no choice for a happier tomorrow. Their faith in their ability to create their own future is gone. The few moments of pleasure they enjoy are seen only as temporary, and even during these brief times they see little hope. The key is to build sufficient internal strength and confidence so that eventually they can handle their own problems.

Once the lows in a person's life get above the "faith in myself" level, as shown in Figure 7, then he can function on his own.

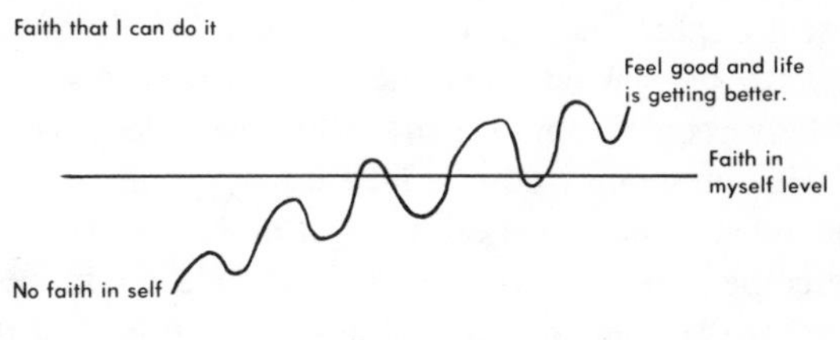

Figure 7

If you are below the "faith in myself" level, then you need a supportive friend or competent counselor. You may be unable, on your own, to develop the confidence and strength needed to change your behavior and improve your life. But as you move above the "faith in myself" level, you will gain enough internal confidence to function well without the need or help of friends and professional counselors.

Many people have said, "You don't understand. I want to be happy, but I can't seem to change. I'm so depressed all the time." Or "I'm sick." "My migraines are back." "My nerves are killing me." "I can't do that because my stomach will be upset all day if I do." "I have an ulcer." "My back aches." "My diarrhea is back again." In essence these are people who have immobilized themselves and who watch the good things in life pass them by.

After many years of counseling people, I believe there are two basic reasons why people do not change: they are afraid the change might be for the worse; and it is easier to remain the same. It takes hard work to do something new and different.

The change is to venture into the unknown. Most of us are fearful and uncertain about the unknown. If we could be guaranteed that the change would be for the better, we might be able to persuade ourselves to try new things. How many people do you know who would not dare to try to change anything but who will complain about their present plight? They have excuses like, "Well, that's the breaks," or, "What rotten luck."

Many people want to change their lives. How to do it is the big question. I have helped many people to change their lives and conquer all kinds of problems. They have overcome unbelievable hurdles they could not master on their own. In helping them, I noticed that most of these people seem to have one thing in common. When they first come in, they are so overwhelmed with problems that they do not know where to begin. They are inundated with every kind of trouble and problem. They look at their life in the same way that Charlie once saw his. Charlie was a client of mine about a year ago. Initially, he saw his life as represented in Figure 8.

He was just swamped. He did not know where to begin. "What's the use?" he said. "I have no control. If it's not one thing, it's another."

People like Charlie seldom know what to do to find success and happiness. After a while, they get to a point where they do not want to try anything because of all their past failures and feelings of inadequacy. That is one reason they never find a better life—they do not begin

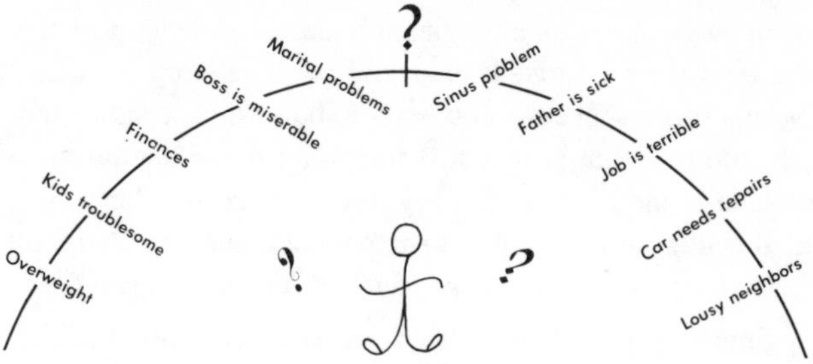

Figure 8

anywhere. The problems in their lives just continue to grow and multiply.

Since they see their problems confronting them all at once, their life becomes overwhelming. Everything looks impossible. Solutions seem impractical because there is a reason why each problem cannot be overcome. Their frustrations grow and this further increases their difficulty in making wise choices.

Personal problems are solved much more easily when we take them one at a time. Once you have solved one problem, the next one seems easier. You always begin by selecting a very small, very specific item in your life that you want to change. The sum of all the small changes makes up a new way of life. It is also important for you to begin by selecting the easiest problem you want to solve or at least to pick one which you think is possible to solve.

Never start with the impossible. Otherwise it is much more difficult to build any self-confidence. Stay away from tackling gigantic problems right off the bat. Some people say, "Let's start with a big one. If we can conquer that problem, the others have to be easy." So they start off with their most difficult problem; such an approach will almost always fail.

Success in solving one small problem after another eventually gives us enough faith and confidence to solve the bigger problems. It is an old but true story—success breeds more success. You want to build on successes, not on failures. That is why it is important in the beginning to choose something at which you can succeed. The secret, in the beginning, is just to experience success. *It is not important what you succeed at but that you succeed.*

Charlie got started on his road to success by attacking his problem at work. He had not been getting along with his foreman at the plant. Maybe one solution was to get to work a little earlier. His boss always seemed easier to get along with when he arrived early rather than late.

Although Charlie's goal was to change his life, his first step was to change what he was doing at work. The idea was to get to work fifteen minutes early every day for one week. Even when we decide to solve a small problem, we often use "overkill" and try big solutions to small problems. Limit your goals. Try to keep things in perspective. It also reinforces your self-image, and the successes feel good week after week.

For Charlie, even his easiest problem was no pushover. Getting to work early was not easy, but, compared to his other problems, it was one he thought he could handle.

How did Charlie get up earlier? He put his alarm clock in the bathtub and set the alarm bell so it would ring as loudly as possible. When it went off, Charlie said, no one could sleep through the racket it made. After a few minutes of that noise, he just had to get up and turn the alarm off.

Once he was in the bathroom, he would splash a little water on his face, and then he was awake. He would get ready for work and leave early. He was the kind of person who, once he got up, he was on his way. Charlie's boss could not believe the transformation. He commented to him about his early arrivals. The following week and the week thereafter, Charlie kept getting to work early. The relationship between Charlie and his foreman became better and better.

This worked so well for Charlie that he suggested to one of his golfing buddies that he come in for counseling. This fellow, a middle-aged man, was a hard worker and very active in community clubs and social organizations. But Gene did not spend much time with his children. He said he wanted to, but he was always on the go, too busy. So Gene's problem was to improve his relationship with his children.

As we discussed his home situation, he said that his kids like to go bowling. There was a bowling alley in one of the shopping malls near their home. So his first plan was to take the kids bowling Sunday afternoons for several weeks. Then we would meet again and see how things were going. After a few weeks, Gene said he had become closer to his kids because of their bowling trips. They had more to talk about. They could talk about bowling styles, their scores, what happened at the alley, and all kinds of things related to the sport. It opened up a whole new way for Gene to become involved with his children.

Thus both Gene and Charlie were able to make changes, but it is not always that easy. The ability to change your life in whatever way you desire basically comes from your own internal strength, in the way outlined in Figure 9.

What helps to develop internal strength and self-confidence is the realization that another person cares. As people start to do things which others see value in, they begin to change their opinion of themselves. A young child holds his mother's hand tightly as he approaches school on his first day of kindergarten. A few days later, he can go by himself. In the adult world, a friend can tem-

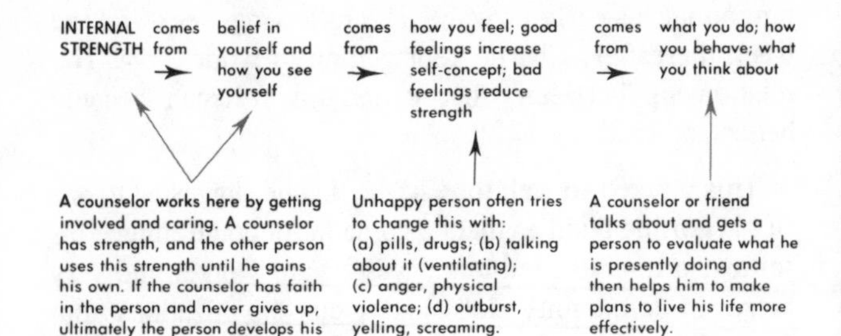

Figure 9

porarily become another person's strength, helping him to develop his own strength and confidence.

In selecting a problem to work on and trying to change your life, it is essential to make a "Do Plan," as Charlie and Gene did. In a Do Plan you must first examine your present behavior. You look at yourself, not at anybody else. You can only control what you do. You can't change others. Then you ask yourself if what you are doing is helping you.

As you evaluate your life, look only at your present or recent behavior. Is what you are doing helping you or anyone else? Don't look into the remote past. And don't worry about what you think you might do in the distant future. Don't search for the reasons why you did certain things. You are looking at human behavior, which cannot be analyzed and classified like a chemical substance. The important thing is that you want to change something you are doing now.

To implement a Do Plan, remember to pick a very small, specific item you want to change. Jotting down your plan in writing is important. It helps you to focus on exactly what it is you are trying to accomplish and shows you really mean business. Make sure your Do Plan is detailed and complete. No loose ends! It is as if you were writing a script for a play and were writing out exactly what the actors should do in one scene. Some Do Plans could even include tentative dialogue, but that is not necessary.

These Do Plans are always based upon positive behavior. Never write a negative Do Plan because they do not work well. For instance, if a young man wanted to get along better with his college roommate, he might write down: "Everyday next week when I come back from classes, I'll smile and say hello as I enter the room." This is a small but specific Do Plan. It is very short in duration and is something any person can do. It is not a negative plan like, "When I see him, I'm not going to argue." All such a negative plan does is keep the word "argue" on your mind.

Putting your goals in positive terms always makes them easier to remember. A person who plans not to drink alcohol would be better off to make a Do Plan about what he is going to do instead, such as, "I'll take a soft drink," or "I'll go out with a friend who knows my problem and will help me avoid doing things that will lead to drinking." A negative plan creates a vacuum in your life which has to be filled with something. Substituting a positive, planned course of action for the behavior you want to avoid is a good technique.

Another part of a Do Plan is to establish a repetitive routine. Whatever it is that you intend to change has undoubtedly been a part of your life for some time. And since changing anything usually takes time, it is important to make a plan that is repetitive. Bad habits are hard to erase. In choosing something you want to change, it is better if you pick something you can work at frequently, every day or maybe every other day. Stay away from sporadic efforts. If a person's goal was to be nice to his girl friend, buying her flowers on her birthday is a great idea, but her birthday comes only once a year, so how much value can that be in building their day-to-day relationship?

A Do Plan should also involve actions of short duration. That improves your chances of success. Later on, you can plan longer actions. But little things like a smile or saying hello in a pleasant manner are all short in terms of time. "Forever plans" such as "I'm never going to do that again as long as I live," may be noble in intention, but they do not work.

To make any Do Plan work, you must be the one to do it. A plan that depends upon another person for success is not the best kind of plan. Your chances of success are greater if you can do it yourself.

One client told me recently that his Do Plan was to be nice to his wife *if* she had dinner ready when he got home. This is a contingency plan. It is contingent upon something his wife has to do. A better plan would have been for him to think of something he could do himself. He could have planned to mix drinks for the two of them and then talk a little before dinner, or maybe take her out to dinner. He could have made dinner. These are avenues where he could channel his own efforts and energies. As his wife sees him trying to work at the relationship, she will be more inclined to work at it, too. Things will get better for both of them.

There are six elements of a good Do Plan.

1. *Small* It is manageable, both in terms of time and what you are going to do.
2. *Specific* It is definite and detailed; it is something you can visualize yourself doing.
3. *Reasonable* It makes sense; you see value in doing it.
4. *Positive* It is *not* what you are not going to do; it *is* what you are going to do.

5. *Repetitive* It is something you can do fairly often.
6. *Independent* It is not dependent on what someone else does.

Don't underestimate the power of putting your Do Plan in writing. Whenever you put something in writing, it seems to have more significance. One technique is to make a chart stating your objective and showing how well you are doing. This is like a progress report on a small part of your life.

As one lonely young college student said, "Putting it in writing brings your actions right out in the open where you can see what you are doing." He was an out-of-state student and did not know anyone in the area. It was too far and too expensive for him to go home on weekends, and he was very lonely in a strange town with no friends. Figure 10 shows some of the Do Plans we worked out.

DO-PLAN	March										
	1	2	3	4	5	6	7	8	9	10	11
Smile and say hello to at least one person in each class	√	√									
Have lunch with someone you know in the cafeteria each day	√	√									
Volunteer to help every Monday evening in the student tutoring program in the English Department	√										

Figure 10

An elderly widow who was very lonely worked out the Do Plans in Figure 11.

I have a friend who ran a highly successful summer theater for twenty years. She told me that making plans was a big part of her success. "You set a definite goal and then you work at it until you achieve it," she said. Then

Do Plan	March										
	1	2	3	4	5	6	7	8	9	10	11
Go to the weekly senior citizens' meeting at city hall and talk to others there; play cards there	√										
Call one friend on the phone each day	√	√	√	√	√						
Volunteer to work on a telephone hotline to talk to people who are troubled			√		√						
Go to church each week and participate in the adult Bible study class				√							
Ask a friend or neighbor over to dinner once a week					√						

Figure 11

she added, "And when problems arise, you face them one at a time. You keep planning and reevaluating, but you never give up." What great advice on how to build a happy and fulfilling life.

Chapter four

Building a relationship

The first time two people meet, a certain kind of "chemistry" begins to work. They either move toward each other or away from each other. Some call this compatibility or physical attraction. Some call it "relating to others." What it is called is not really important. What is important is being aware of how this interaction works. This is especially important for someone who is lonely and looking for friends.

When two people meet, the greater the attraction they have for each other, the faster they would like to move toward more involvement with each other. I call this the "speed"* of the relationship. It accelerates or decelerates as the relationship itself increases or decreases.

A good example of how speed works is to look at what happens when a boy meets a girl. It feels good just to talk. Later, on a date, they hold hands. That feels even better. As the couple continues to move toward each other, they kiss. That tingles the nervous system even more. Excitement. Newness. It feels great. The speed of their relationship is accelerating and that always feels good. As they grow more intimate with each other, their feelings grow

---

*See *The Identity Society* by Dr. William Glasser, pp. 70-71.

more intense and highly pleasurable. The faster this happens, the greater the speed of the relationship.

Some relationships have high speed at the beginning but nothing later on. Speed is largely based on physical attraction and the newness that exists between two people. That is one reason why it does not last. You can come only so close to someone and then the feelings of newness and the thrill of getting to know the person will begin to attenuate. The speed of the relationship begins to decelerate.

The feelings of a decelerating relationship are always unpleasant. Everyone wants to feel good; and when the relationship is on the decline, they feel bad. It is much harder to sustain the relationship when there are not many good feelings between two people.

Speed demands variety to keep it going, and variety comes in many ways. You can find speed in a variety of friends or you can find variety with one friend by doing different things together. Most love relationships are started by the speed—the attraction two people have for each other. It is not hard for most people to start a relationship. *What is hard is to keep a relationship going after the speed is gone.*

Another aspect in interpersonal relationships is quality. Quality is simply the value you ascribe to the other person. It is not only physical appearance that makes up quality, it is personality, mannerisms, ideas, the way that a person comes across to you. Quality is the total person. Of course, the quality we place on someone varies with our own point of view. What one person thinks is quality often does not mean much to another.

The real key to building a lasting relationship is not speed or quality; it is depth. The depth of a relationship is the degree to which two people have built relational strength from doing things together that take effort, things that are enjoyable and active. That is the way to build strength into a relationship so that it doesn't fall apart in times of stress.

Relationships that last show a great deal of depth because the people involved do things together that they enjoy. The three components of speed, quality, and depth are divided approximately as shown in Figure 12. It is the depth that keeps the relationship going, makes it enjoyable, and, more important, builds the relational strength into it.

On the other hand, a relationship that does not last looks like Figure 13. The speed cannot sustain the relationship for long. Without depth or strength, the relationship will die or wane away into nothing.

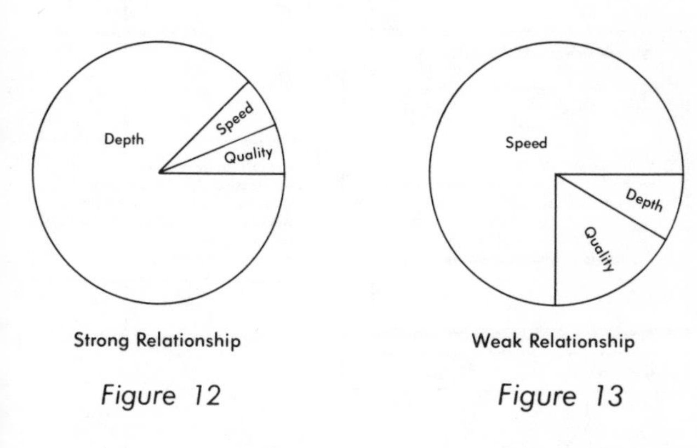

Strong Relationship

Figure 12

Weak Relationship

Figure 13

One of the best signs of two people being happy together is that they laugh a lot. They enjoy being with each other. The reason laughter is so good for a relationship is that it almost magically breaks down any tension between two people. Laughter quickly dissipates antagonism. It feels good to laugh. It is hard to stay angry at someone when you are laughing together. *Laughter turns hate to love quicker than anything I know.*

Friends who never laugh when they are together do not have much of a relationship. There seems to be something missing. They do not appear to be happy. Some couples even eat in silence in restaurants. It is hard to understand what goes on in such relationships. Figure 14 gives a schematic representation of how strong relationships are developed.

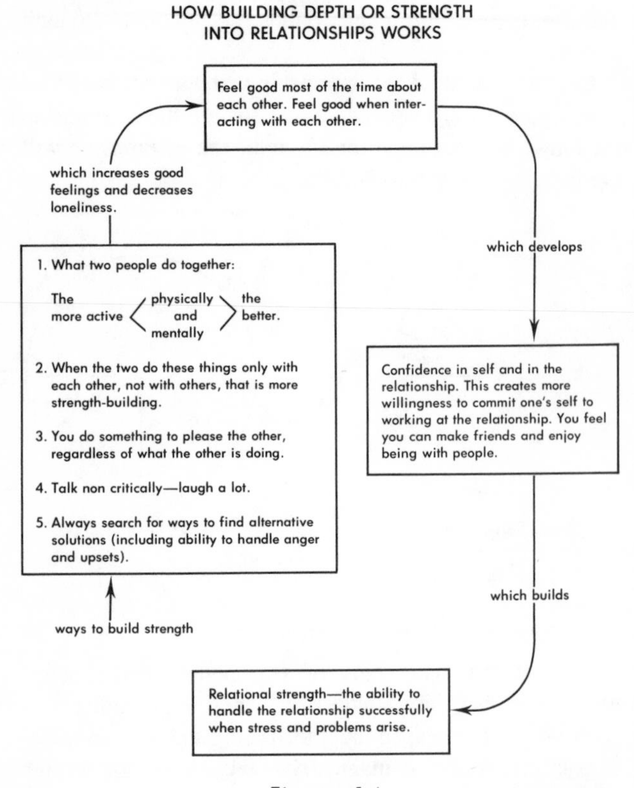

Figure 14

One of the steps in maintaining a good relationship is learning how to cope with anger. Many people cannot handle their anger. They fly off the handle at the slightest provocation. They get upset and say things they do not mean. Their anger makes others uncomfortable and leads to alienation and loneliness.

Successful people learn very early in life that they cannot build many friendships unless they learn to control their anger. No matter how much you want to tell someone off, it is usually best if you do not. It never does any good. You have to ask yourself whether the relationship will be better if you tell the other person off or if you keep your composure.

What does it mean when you really get angry with a friend or someone you love? It sometimes means that you doubt that the other person really cares about you. Your mind reasons: "If he really cared about me, he would have been more thoughtful"; or, "If she really loved me, she'd never do that." The closer the relationship, the more it hurts when anything is done that can be interpreted as a personal rejection.

Often we expect too much from a relationship and read into it more than is really there. These false assumptions can quickly lead to anger unless we take the time to talk things over. It is when we let anger control us that we hit someone or throw the good china or slam our fist on the table or scream four-letter words at the top of our lungs.

Anger mainly tells us we are not working hard enough at getting along with the other person. Anger means we have to use our brains to figure out something more positive to do than getting angry.

Remember, we have control over how we feel through what we do. If we know and feel someone does not care about us or if we know someone *does* care about us, but we do not have the *feeling* they do, we can change that feeling. How? By trying to do something to move toward them in a relational or caring way.

We love others for our own sake, not for theirs. It is we who gain when we are kind and caring toward another. We grow to love others more as we work at loving them. For others to be happy with us, they in turn have to work at loving us. We form relationships because we need someone to work at loving. Anger tells us we are not working hard enough.

The wife of a good friend of mine has all too often burned food on the stove. This still happens rather frequently. About every other month, the food is burned so badly that it ruins a pan. My friend used to get very angry when this happened and would rant and rave, but the food would still be burned. After a while, he realized that getting angry did not keep the food from getting burnt. All it did was reduce the happiness in the house.

Finally, he concluded that the best thing to do was to figure the cost of a new pan into the monthly budget. The children also agreed to help by checking the stove, which further reduced the loss of pots and pans. In fact, the family laughs about the subject now.

Anger has to be handled by the angry person. Anger is a sign of his inability to work at a relationship. It is the worst way to handle frustration. Anger and upset can also become an excuse for not accepting the responsibility to work at a relationship. Anger, in a sense, is a tool the anger-prone person uses to manipulate others: "Please don't do anything to irritate Dad tonight. He's in a bad mood;" or "Tom gets angry, so no one play the radio loudly;" or "My roommate is tired and angry today, so everyone try to do whatever she wants."

Anger usually results in one of three courses of behavior (see Figure 15). The first is physical. Throwing things and hitting people are examples of this type of behavior. A second recourse is to lash out verbally. That is when people say a lot of inconsiderate, mean things they would not otherwise say. A third alternative is the silent treatment. Angry people become sulky and will not talk to those they are upset with. They will talk to others but according to their own rules. They may be fine at work or anywhere else in public, but at home they are a terror. Their logic is simple; there is no use pouting and giving the silent treatment unless it is in front of those who made them angry. They need an audience, and they have a particular audience in mind.

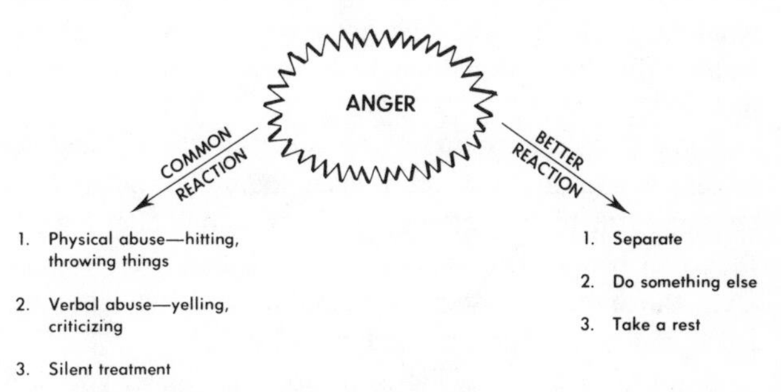

Figure 15

None of these alternatives truly relieves the pain of anger any more than yelling about how hungry you are relieves hunger pains. All anger really tells you is that something is wrong. You still have to figure out what to do to correct the situation.

What we should do is to separate from the person with whom we are angry and turn to something else. At this point, the relationship is too fragile to handle the stress of the problem. Separation gives each person time to calm down, to unwind, to gain strength. Also, an argument is avoided, which in turn will help us improve the relationship with the other person. No one loses and everyone wins. Anger always diminishes in time. No one stays angry for long. The best course of action, then, is to do something else for a while. Anything physical—running, exercising, scrubbing the floor—is good.

Remember, to change how you feel you have to first change what you are doing. Sitting there all alone, depressed and remorseful, because of what you said in the haste of anger, will not help you feel better. That is only a form of self-punishment. You want to feel good, but instead you feel guilty. Sometimes that leads to even further anger. One of my friends has a boy of about sixteen who lifts weights every time he gets angry with his two little brothers. Until he and his mother figured out what he could do when he got angry, he would hit his smaller brothers and the whole house would be in an uproar.

Some people may find rest is a better way of handling anger. A nap or a hot bath relaxes them. The behavior is changed, the feeling ultimately changes, and after a while they feel better. The important thing is that they separate from those they are angry with and calm down. Then the issue can be encountered and resolved.

Building a close relationship does not mean you will always agree with your companion. If you want to be well liked, this does not mean you should have no opinions of your own. You are entitled to your ideas, but you should listen thoughtfully to the other so that, if you do differ, you will be able to look for alternatives. If you do that, you will keep the argument and disagreements to a minimum. The two of you will keep moving toward each other as you share bits and pieces of your lives.

When people say things you do not agree with, you do not have to disagree openly. Just listen to their ideas. They are entitled to that, as much as you are. It is certainly all right for people to disagree. It's a shame more people do not realize this.

Learning how to conduct a good conversation is just as important in building a relationship as learning what to do when you are angry. People who find it hard to communicate are usually lonely. There are four guidelines to pleasant conversation.

1. Be nonjudgmental. Reserve your judgment until the other person has finished his point. Don't start shaking your head "no" even before he has finished.

2. Listen intelligently and thoughtfully to what the other person is saying. Being a good listener means paying attention. Look at the person you are talking to. You may want to repeat their position in your own words to show you understand.

3. Don't rush things. If you disagree, think about a few alternatives before responding negatively. This enables people to enjoy talking to you. Also, it lets you talk about a lot more things. Nobody likes to talk to a person with a closed mind.

4. If what is said is agreeable to you, then it is a simple matter to move forward in harmony and agreement. But let the other person know what you think. Call your conversation partner by name, too.

When Alice, a high school senior, would come home from school and try to talk to her mother about what she wanted to do after graduation, her mother would say, "I don't want to talk about it. You know your father and I don't approve of your getting any job until you've gone to college at least two years." But Alice did not want to go to college; she wanted to be a dental technician.

Her mother would "tune her out," by turning on the TV or by talking to Alice's dad. Somethines her mother would go into another room right in the middle of the conversation. So Alice turned to other people to talk to about her future. She talked with friends at school and several of her favorite teachers.

When Alice's mother went to a PTA meeting one night, one of the biology teachers mentioned Alice's ability in science and her desire to be a dental technician. He commented how well she should do in that field. Alice's mother went home furious. "She talks to everyone but us," she said to her husband.

Many parents talk to their children but not about things the children are interested in discussing. And lots of parents and children do not talk very much at all, even though they live in the same house. They are almost strangers. Deep down, they love each other; but they have not developed an ability to discuss things together. They are reluctant "to put themselves out"—to take the time and energy to develop relationships.

Parents come in for counseling and say, "I'd like to talk with my kids, but we don't have much to say to each other." After talking to them for just a few minutes, it is obvious how busy they are and how busy their children are, too. They have a million things they could discuss and share with each other, but they do not know how to go about it. The parents are lonely, and the children are lonely. They have each other and are so close—yet so far. They do not know how to communicate. When they try, the result is often an argument and disagreement.

In an attempt to avoid arguments, many people decide they will make no value judgments at all. Such people are so nonjudgmental that they are frustrating to be with. You ask them, "Who do you think will run for President?" and they reply, "I have no idea." The person who tries not to voice his opinion usually does so because he does not want to offend anyone by taking an opposite view. The only problem with that approach is that it does not help bring people closer together. If several friends are talking together, it does not help the group discussion if one of them never voices any opinions. Talking is fun, but you sometimes have to work at it.

People can grow closer together if they want to. Loneliness can be overcome by an enjoyable conversation.

Searching for alternatives is a delightful form of creativity and should not be considered as compromising. The broadening of options through communication brings spice and zest to life. It requires thinking. Many times alternatives turn out to be more enjoyable than the original plans, and these pleasant surprises are a great source of joy.

It is also important in building any type of relationship that judgment be rendered only after the relationship has gained enough strength to handle it. You would not say things on a first date that you would after five years of marriage, because the relationship at the dating stage could not handle it. It would end the relationship right there. But several years later, the same thing can be said without any devastating effects.

The use of insulting language such as, "You're dumb," or "That's the stupidest thing you've ever said," is certainly not conducive to building a good relationship. Statements such as, "You're weird," or "You idiot, you're just like your mother (or father or whoever)," cast doubt upon the self-image of the person who is on the receiving end of these barbs. These "killer" statements quickly undermine a close relationship. If a lonely person decides to give this kind of treatment to others, he winds up lonelier than ever. *Nothing turns love to hate as quickly as criticism.*

Belittling, putting someone down verbally, and ridiculing all amount to the same thing. They are ways of verbally subjecting the other person to degradation and of destroying a relationship.

When Debbie and Patty, two young divorcees, first began living together, they used to spend a great deal of time talking about all kinds of things. One night Debbie mentioned a problem with her boss at work. Patty was highly critical of her for being upset with her boss. So

Debbie stopped talking about her boss. Then one time Patty mentioned something about what one of her friends at work was doing on weekends, and Debbie got upset. Patty stopped talking about this friend and the other friends she had at the office. Another time Debbie was complaining about her mother, and Patty was critical of her again.

What was happening to Patty and Debbie happens to many people. It is simply that any time a person finds it difficult to talk with someone about something, he or she avoids that topic. After a while, Debbie and Patty did not talk much because they were afraid that every time they opened their mouths they would be criticized. As the months went on, they talked less and less to each other.

How to get conversations going and keep them going is important. Most conversations start with a question such as, "How are you?" "What's new?" and so on. Questions with one-word replies should be avoided if your goal is to get a discussion going. If you say, "Did you like the movie?" and they say, "No," where do you go from there? The best questions are open ended. You do not have to show great intelligence to ask these questions. Questions which ask for many different answers are good, such as, "What scenes from the movie did you enjoy?" or, "Tell me some of the things you did when. . . ." Also, questions which ask an opinion are most helpful in discussions. "What do you think of the current economic situation?" "Why is country music your favorite?"

Often the most enjoyable conversations come from questions that require thought. "How else would you have ended the movie to make it more enjoyable?" "What kind of person would you add to the story to make it more amusing?" Whenever creative and imaginative questions are asked, the conversation is stimulating. A creative interchange is always enjoyable.

Whether you are lonely or not, if you want to improve your relationships, you have to learn the art of conversation. You have to learn how to enjoy talking with others and what to do to make it easier for them to enjoy talking with you. Improving conversational skills takes constant effort. To be interesting you must have something to say. Personal and intellectual growth and vitality contribute immensely.

As a close relationship begins to break down and deteriorate, talking becomes less pleasant and less frequent. When this starts to happen, we respond by feeling bad, and whenever we feel bad we tend to blame whomever we are involved with for our bad feelings. Many people enter into relationships and end them very quickly because they never build the strength necessary to handle the stress of bad feelings.

There are definite signs to look for in the breakdown of a relationship. We first begin to question what the other person is doing—either in our mind, privately, to ourselves, or openly to the other person. Second, we then try to change our partner by discussions or indirect means. If this does not work, usually we resort next to criticism, perhaps openly. Criticism always hurts and seldom, if ever, helps a relationship. Criticism erodes self-confidence and weakens the very relationship two people are trying to build. One of the keys to a successful life is to stop being overly critical of yourself and others around you. The only time criticism should be used is if it is about something over which the person has control. Past actions or physical traits should not be criticized.

The fourth stage of the decline of a relationship comes as criticisms give way to outward verbal abuse, physically striking out in anger, or complete indifference. These stages are danger signals to people that they had better try something else. Building and maintaining a relationship is crucial if loneliness is to be overcome and any lasting sense of happiness is to be gained.

On the other hand, there are probably many relationships that should be aborted simply because of basic incompatibility and lack of common interests. I think it is a virtue to sense when this is the case and to quit pretending. I know of one such instance in which two older men, in their haste to rid themselves of loneliness, took up living together. They had little in common, but in hopes of improving their lot they moved in together, thinking it would work out. Their personalities clashed, the relationship was a terrible one. In fact, all they had in common was loneliness. What they did not have was the knowledge of how to get along.

Chapter five

Where to find friends

You cannot make friends if you are sitting home alone watching TV, or knitting all by yourself in a corner somewhere. It is easy to get started on the way to friendship, if you really want to have friends. The world is full of friendly people.

Some people feel that it is not easy to make friends. They view the world as full of cold, indifferent people. To prove their point, they refer to all the people who walk past each other and do not say hello or give a nod of recognition.

Such people do not realize that you see what you want to see. It is all up to you. Smile, and people smile back. Say hello, and most people will say hello right back to you. Soon you can be involved—if you want to be. And you must be willing to be hurt sometimes. People, by their nature, want to be friendly. They learn not to be friendly from bad experiences.

Reaching out to others may take a little effort, but the friendship you receive in return is well worth it. To love is really the greatest risk. The first order of business is to go where there are people, and these people should be considered potential friends. How can that be? How can strangers be potential friends? It is easy, if you have things in common with them. A basic ingredient of all friendships is doing things in common.

Just think of something you like to do, perhaps a hobby or something you have always wanted to learn. It does not matter whether it is a physical or a mental activity, but it should be an involving type of activity. It should not be something you do alone, hidden in the privacy of your own home, unless you are able to share the fruits of that activity with others.

Part of the fun in collecting anything is showing your collection to others. Real joy comes in sharing. Part of the fun in doing something like boating is being with people who like the same things you do. These activities by their nature involve you with others with whom you are most likely to find interests in common. You develop a sense of belonging. You feel accomplishment as others see value in what you do.

You find friends more easily when you do something others also enjoy doing. There are many things to look forward to with anticipation. Activities you can dig into and lose yourself in are the best. The more you can throw yourself into an activity, the better. To forget about your worries and enjoy being with others, you have to be enthusiastic about something outside yourself. Depressed people focus in. Happy people focus out.

Think back to the last time you really enjoyed yourself. Were you thinking of yourself and all your troubles while you were having this good time? Of course not. To enjoy yourself, you forget about yourself. It is kind of a paradox, but it is true. You get together with a lot of people and have fun, and the time is gone before you know it. That is the type of activity you want to look for.

The real key in building strength into a relationship is that the activity should involve some degree of effort. Pleasure received without effort does nothing to help an individual gain strength or a friendship grow strong (see Figure 16).

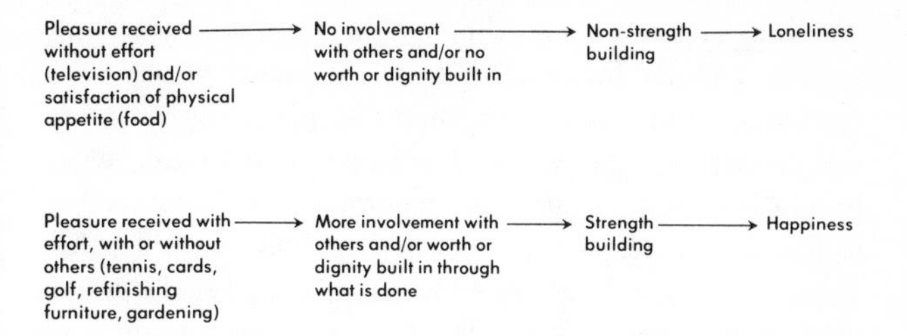

Figure 16

If you want to be with people and if you like boating, you go to a marina. If you like skiing or bowling, you go where there are ski lodges or bowling alleys. If you like flying, take flying lessons. If you like photography, go to a camera shop and join a club. Once you do that, then what? Don't stand around watching others and waiting to get involved. If you are lonely and hurting inside, all that would do is make you feel more miserable. Come alive. You must risk the uncertainty of beginning something new.

After you arrive at a place where there are activities you like, how do you make friends? There is no single answer to that question because we all make friends in our own particular way. In essence, this whole book is talking about how to get involved and make friends. Some people make friends very quickly and some take longer.

We meet lots of people every day. We are introduced and we shake hands, but these people are just acquaintances. The difference between a friendship and an acquaintance is that a friendship endures and has depth. Friends are people you care about and spend time with. You share your joy and build your strength. Acquaintances are people you just know, and that is about all there is to the relationship.

How does an acquaintance become a friend? Well, for one thing, it takes time. Although there is much more to it, time is a major factor. The basic soundness of any relationship is built and strengthened as people spend more and more time together. A friendship, when it starts out, is in a rather fragile stage. The important thing to remember in finding friends is to get out and to "put yourself out."

Sally wandered into the office one day and said she was looking for help. She was about twenty-two and her husband had been killed in an auto accident six months earlier. She was having a tough time getting over it emotionally. She had a small child with her, a boy about two years old. She said she felt so down and depressed that she did not even want to get out of bed. She said she did not even know how she made it to the office.

We talked for a while about her life and what she liked to do. At first she said, "Nothing. Nothing interests me any more." So we shifted to what she liked to do before she got married. She said she enjoyed outdoor things like bicycling and tennis. She had not been bicycling since she got married, and the last time she played tennis was before she became pregnant.

We called a local bicycle dealer, and he gave us the names of several bicycle clubs in the area. One of the clubs met in a nearby park. We called the park superintendent, and he gave us the time and place of the next club meeting. She went to the meeting that weekend, which was good since weekends are usually worse when you are lonely. She got to know some of the members of the club and made a few friends.

The club bicycled over nature trails in the park to various locations and then did a little birdwatching. Sally did not know much about that, but she said it was fun. She had become involved, and had an activity that brought her into contact with others. She had to work at making friends. It did not happen overnight. But she was not sitting around the apartment all day feeling sorry for herself. She started to feel good about herself again.

If you are trying to help someone who is withdrawn and lonely, don't give him or her advice like, "You should join a bridge club and play cards. You'll really enjoy yourself." Although this may be a good suggestion, such advice usually falls on deaf ears. People have good intentions and would like to do what friends and relatives have suggested. But somehow they never get around to it. They know it would help and you know it would help, but what happens? They do not have the internal strength to move toward others. If you really want to help, you will have to lend them some of your strength.

This can be done by getting yourself in the picture. You get involved with the person until he or she can get involved with others. Try saying something like, "Let's go to the village card club this Wednesday. I'll pick you up at 8:00." Now that is a definite time and a definite card club. Because you have said you will go with them, the chances of getting them out of their shell are much greater. Furthermore, when you go with that person, even if it is just for the first couple of times, your interest in them greatly enhances their ability to find more friends and get rid of the pain found in loneliness.

Finding enjoyable things to do with others that can be repeated is one of the keys to overcoming loneliness. There is some value in attending one or two bridge-club meetings. To get the maximum effect, you have to get involved in activities which you do regularly. The regular contact and constant involvement in enjoyable activities enables a person to build the strength needed to get over depression and the time needed to build meaningful relationships.

What many people do not understand about loneliness is that it is not like an occasional headache that can be cured by a couple of aspirins. It does not go away because of one or two phone calls. One night out on the town does not last very long.

Lonely people are not helped very much by one or two visits each month. Granted, they may cheer up briefly, and sometimes that is better than nothing. But some people get even more depressed and sink deeper into loneliness after an occasional visit by a friend or relative. The person may feel so good being with someone for a change that they realize how lonely they have been.

When people do things together, it is important that they do things which strengthen their relationship so it can handle stress. Passive activities such as watching a movie or TV together do not strengthen a relationship. Physical activities, like camping, tennis, swimming, and bowling are much more effective in building depth into friendships. Bridge, Scrabble, and Monopoly are examples of mental activities that strengthen relationships.

Close friendships are not developed in a crowd. Couples who go out with other couples often do not spend much time with each other during the evening. If they interact with many other couples, it tends to water down the relation-strengthening process and thus no building occurs. They do not have to work as hard at getting along with each other because there are so many others around. Close friendships are developed in one-to-one encounters. Doing things alone with another is very strengthening.

It is important that your friends have at least some of the same interests you have. The more interests you have in common, the more things you can do together and the better your chances are for building a good relationship. That is why interest groups are so helpful in finding friends.

To help people find interesting things to do, I have compiled a rather lengthy list of activities which are enjoyable and offer involvement. They're all very active pursuits. The list is meant to be all-inclusive. Passive activities, although interesting to some people, were purposely not included since they do not provide as much opportunity for building and maintaining friendships.

A

Agricultural hobbies and clubs
Airplanes
- models
- schools or learn-to-fly groups
- charter and rental clubs

All-terrain vehicles (ATVs)
Amateur radio operators
Amateur theater
Amusement Parks
Animals
- pets
- kennels
- shows and clubs

Antiques
- repair and restoring

Appliances
- fix-it shops (Swap shops)

Aquatics
Aquariums
Archery
Archaeology
Art galleries and societies
Art
Astrology
Astronomy
Athletics
- clubs
- games

Auctions
Automobile
- body work and custom finishing
- racing
- sports cars
- clubs of all types (antique cars, sports cars)

B

Backpacking
Baking
Badminton
Ballet
Bands
Baseball
Basketball
Baton twirling
Bazaars
Belly dancing
Bible schools or clubs
Bicycling
- clubs
- trails

Big-band clubs and record clubs
Billiards
Bingo
Birds
- pets
- birdwatching

Blind organizations
- volunteer work

Boarding
- dogs, cats

Boats
Books
- clubs
- libraries

Botanical gardens
Boutiques
Bowling
Boy Scouts
Bridge
Broadcasting
Building
- (just about anything here)

Business
- schools
- do-it-yourself projects

Bus rides and travel
Butterfly collections

C

Cake decorating
Camera
- exchanges
- clubs
- photography

Camp Fire Girls
Camping
Candle making
Canoeing
Cards
Cats
Caves
Cement work
Ceramics
Charitable organizations
- volunteer work

Child care
Chinaware
Chess
Church work
Citizens' radio
Civil defense
  volunteer work
Coins
Collections
  (everything from soup to nuts)
College
Computers
Crocheting
Croquet
Cruises

D

Dancing
  folk
  modern
  square
Darts
Decoupage
Diaries
Diving
  skin
  scuba
Diet clubs
  weight-watchers
Dogs
Drawing
Dressmaking
Dune buggies

E

Ecology clubs and projects
Electric trains
Embroidery
Engraving
ESP
European cars
Exercise programs

F

Fabrics
Farming
Fencing
Festivals
Field hockey
First-aid classes
Fishing
Flowers
  shows
  clubs
Flying
Food
  gourmet
Football
Frisbee
Framing pictures
Fraternal organizations
Furniture
  design
  repair
  refinishing

G

Games
Gardening
Girl Scouts
Glass-blowing
Gliders
Go-carts
Goldfish
Golf
Greenhouse
Guitar
Guns
Gymnastics

H

Handball
Handicrafts
Health spa
Helicopter
Hi-fi
Hiking
Hitchhiking
Historical society
Hockey
Home building and care
Horses and horseback riding
Horticulture
Hospital
  volunteer work
Houseboat
Hunting

I-J-K

Ice-fishing
Ice-skating
Illustrations
Insect collections
Interior decorating
Iron work
  ornamental
Jewelry
Jogging
Juggling
Journalism
Judo
Karate
Kites
Knitting groups

L-M-N-O

Lacrosse
Lawn care
Leather working
Lettering
  printing
Livery stables
Macrame
Magicians
Mechanical devices-toys
Mini-bikes
Miniature collectors' items
Model building
Modeling clay

Monograms
Mountain climbing
Motion pictures
Motorcycles
Movies
Murals
Museums
Music
Needlepoint
Nursing
Opera
Orchardists
Orchestras
Organs

P-Q-R

Painting
Paddle tennis
Parks
Photography
Physical fitness
Piano
Ping-pong
Planes
  models
  flying lessons
Plants
Plastics
Playgrounds
Pleasure resorts
Politics
Polo
Pool
Puppetry
Puzzles
Quartets
Quilling
Quilting
Racing
Radio
Racquet ball
Rare-book clubs
Reading clubs
Rebuilding engines
Restaurants
Rock collections
Roller-skating
Rug weaving
Running

S-T-U-V

Sailing
School
Sculpting
Sewing
Skeet shooting
Skydiving
Sleigh rides
Soccer
Social work
  volunteer work
Softball
Sororities
Speed boats
Spelunking
Sports cars
Sportsmen clubs
Squash
Stamps
Stereo
Study clubs
Surfing
Sunbathing
Swimming
Tap dancing
Tapes
  audio
  video
Taxidermy
Tennis
Theater
Tiring-(Snow)
Tobogganing
Track meets
Trains
Traveling
Treasure hunting
Tree climbing
Tropical fish
Tubing (rapids)
Tumbling
Tutoring
Upholstering
Visiting shut-ins
Vocalizing
  barber shop quartets
  church choir
  symphony chorus
Volleyball
Volunteer work
Volcanic studies

W-X-Y-Z

Wagoneering
Wallpapering
Water-skiing
Weaving
Weight-lifting
Wildlife
Writing
  autobiography
  books
  diary
  fiction
  letters
  music
  poetry
  reports
Yacht clubs
Yoga
Youth organizations
Zoo
Zoological gardens and clubs

After looking over the list and identifying a number of interesting activities, how do you find out more about them? If you like horses and horseback riding, how do you find out where there are others who share those interest?

I have found three valuable sources for this information: local newspapers, the Yellow Pages of the telephone book, and volunteer organizations. Newspapers always carry announcements about club events and meetings. You can easily look in the Yellow Pages to find the names, addresses, and phone numbers of organizations, clubs, and people associated with particular interests. Volunteer organizations are good places to find friendly people and to fill up your empty hours. Almost every nonprofit group can use another person who is willing to lend a helping hand. And when people are glad to see you, you feel good about being there. They feel good, you feel good, and this is how you can make friends. The hardest move is the first step, and the greatest joy is the journey.

There is a kind of snowball effect. Things just keep rolling along, getting better and better for you. It is also easier to forget about being lonely when you are helping others. Soon you forget about yourself. You are bound to have at least one thing in common with the people you meet in volunteer work—a desire to help others. You will find these organizations will be very friendly and will welcome you with open arms.

The other day, a middle-aged, slightly overweight woman came in for counseling. She was single and lonely. Her only two friends had moved out of town recently. We tried to think of somewhere she could go or something she might do to get involved with others.

Suddenly an idea came to my mind from a newspaper ad about an opening play—our local amateur theater. They do an excellent job of putting on plays and are always looking for people to work both on and off stage.

After a few calls, Betty was on her way. She literally went directly from the office to the playhouse, and everything went well. She fit in beautifully. She had met a lot of people, had a date for the coming weekend, and seemed to be well on her way. Obviously, few people improve that quickly, but Betty already had some degree of strength and needed only a little direction.

You would be surprised how many times these three sources—the phone book, the newspaper, and a volunteer organization—have helped people find friends and overcome loneliness. People are out there, but you have to reach out.

Chapter six

Time and money

Most of us feel we would not be lonely if we had enough money to do anything we wanted. On the other hand, many people with money are lonely simply because they have too much time on their hands. Not enough money, too much money. Not enough time, too much time. How we spend our time and money really tells us what we are.

What we do during the twenty-four hours in each day determines whether or not we are satisfied with life. Many people do not utilize the time they have in a way that gives them enough sense of value and accomplishment. What they are seeking is their own expectation of what self-fulfillment is, and not what it actually is.

We hear wisecracks about the importance of money such as, "It's way ahead of whatever is in second place," or "Maybe money can't buy happiness, but it sure helps." Everyone knows money cannot actually buy happiness. You cannot buy your way out of loneliness; you have to do something valuable with your time.

One of the real surprises of modern times has been man's failure to satisfactorily adjust to increased leisure time. Leisure is your free or uncommitted time. It is during this time that people want to experience the good feelings of "fun." We often hear the lament, "I wish I had more time off," or, "If I didn't have to work, would I have it made." The people who make such statements are usually very busy people. But confronted with the possibility of leisure, a person who is accustomed to being busy will soon look for something to do. They often become too bored just sitting around.

However, leisure can be what you make it. As long as it is not destructive to you or others, what you do with your free time is up to you. Some people love to use their free time in very passive ways, sitting, relaxing, watching TV.

In my case, I always look forward to leisurely vacations when I can sit on the beach and soak up the sun. But after a while, I find it difficult to just sit around and do nothing. I start to get anxious. I am eager to do something, anything, to be busy. I think man is happiest when he is active. Man is, by nature, a doer. But moderation is the key. Man has to learn to be an enjoyer and to realize that constant activity can be just as destructive as complete passivity.

This is much easier said than done because, when a person is accustomed to a certain amount of activity, his system develops an "activation level." Everyone's mental and physical system is used to a certain amount of energy output. When a person stops this activity, or slows down below his usual energy level, he feels uncomfortable. He has to readjust to a new activation level, and that takes time. When I go on vacation, it takes me a while to unwind and get settled into a slower pace.

The strange part of the current talk about shorter work-weeks and early retirement is that many of those who do retire early do not stop working and many with short working-hours get a second job. Many continue to work on a limited basis. Whether or not people can handle increasing amounts of leisure time is a big factor in loneliness. It appears that the growth in leisure time will continue. In fact, the pursuit of leisure and pleasure is becoming a big business. The post-World War II era brought many new pastimes. The freeways and interstate highways have encouraged more Americans to find leisure through travel. Trailers and campers crowd the highways.

Recreation, including travel, sports, and hobbies, has come into modern American life at an extremely rapid rate. Simultaneously there has been a decrease in working hours. At first, more time for recreation has great appeal. But to many, this increased free time away from the job has become a new cause for boredom and loneliness. How to occupy one's time in a non-self-destructive way has become a new problem for many Americans.

And, as the rubber factories in Akron, Ohio, found out when they tried the short work-week, many didn't work less. They just got second jobs. Some said they needed to work two jobs to keep up with inflation. Others said it was not the money they wanted—it was that working two jobs beat sitting around the house with nothing to do.

On the other hand, many find it difficult to find second jobs, and when unemployment is high some find it difficult to find the first job. Coping with free time during unemployment can be distressing.

Many sit around every night, watching TV endlessly. Their weekends are even worse. Some have tried the long weekend vacation package-trips and have "discovered America," but are still bored. They want something thrilling and enjoyable, something that lasts.

For years, people worked to earn whatever money they needed—money to pay bills, to buy necessary things, and thus to live better and longer. The pursuit was to earn what was needed and to bargain for less hours. What has been happening recently is a startling revelation. Some people achieved a three-day or four-day weekend. Often they are not any happier; they are just bored. They make the same amount of money, yet they are still bored and lonely. Free time, in itself, is not the answer. We seek variety, and when it is not there the end result can be depression and withdrawal.

People get bored doing the same thing over and over, even if what they do is fun. "Let's go see this, and let's go see that." "Should we take a three or five-day trip to Mexico?" "Let's live in California." "Let's play tennis." "How about a movie?" "Let's eat out." We are in pursuit of something. We earn more, we work less, but are we really any happier? Where are we headed? Is this the generation of the alienated? The uninvolved? Do industrial societies, by their nature, create apathy and indifference?

A good friend told me that, as soon as she has learned something, she loses interest and goes on to something else. She does not become very accomplished at it; she learns it because, as she once said, "I just want to know if I can do it." She tried knitting, then decided to quit because, "Now I know I can knit." Since then she has gone from bowling to yoga to tennis. Now she does not know what to do next. Like many I know, she has difficulty finding something that will sustain her interest. The important thing here is to keep looking.

The key to happiness is in what you do with your time. The person who sits around and does not do much will find it all too easy to become depressed and dissatisfied. He spends too much time looking inward at his life, at how he feels and why he is lonely. You do not have to work and be busy all the time. You do have to do things that are worthwhile. *Modern-day people must learn to gain a sense of worth from activities which are relevant to them—whether they be at work or at leisure.*

People want more out of a job today than just a paycheck. They want job satisfaction and a sense of personal accomplishment. This goal is not unique to this generation, but preceding generations of Americans were more concerned with security or mere survival. Earning a living on the farm took all the energies a family could muster. Little thought was given to self-fulfillment. It was not long ago that memories of the Great Depression of the 1930s lingered hauntingly in the back of everyone's mind. Today with energy crises, rising gasoline prices, and spiraling inflation, merely living and holding a job is a major concern. However, there is a difference. In the 1930s, getting laid off or being out of work was the worst thing that could happen to a man and his family because there were no unemployment benefits, no welfare, no food stamps, and no social security. There were only soup lines and emergency help from a few agencies. Although there is still a sense of urgency when one or both parents have been laid off, there is also a certain sense of security. Why? Today no one will starve from a lack of food. People are aware of unemployment benefits. The federal, state, and local governments are there to help, and this "secondary" security has an effect on a person's priorities.

In many plants and factories, management cannot get help to perform dull or menial tasks. Is it because the young workers today are healthier or better educated? I do not think so. I feel there is less concern today about such things as wages, benefits, and job security. Once achieved, these elements are taken for granted.

Young people are sure of some degree of financial security and are more concerned about the circumstances of their job. In work, as in other areas, expectations are higher. They seek and hope for satisfaction on their job because they want to enjoy what they do as well as earn a living. They look for an element of control over their destiny, including their job.

Old-timers will say, "These kids should be glad they have a job." Many young people are not. They care about what they do with their life rather than simply about how much money they can make. There is a big difference between the older people who focus on security and younger people who expect more. The depression generation seeks economic guarantees first and self-fulfillment later. Today's younger generation looks for personal enjoyment and self-fulfillment first because it expects a certain amount of security from the government.

To the older generation, worth and dignity came from having worked hard and successfully raised a family; to the young, what they do—whether the job itself, raising children, or leisure activities—must give dignity and worth, and it must be satisfying.

People caught in repetitive, boring jobs are turning to shorter work-weeks and more leisure as an escape. Our great technological society, built on the old Puritan work ethic, is shifting from a work culture to a leisure culture. The flight from loneliness and boredom is affecting us on the job. Union shop stewards who once spent their time on seniority and security-related matters now concern themselves also with such aspects as boredom. All this is evidence of a shift from a security-oriented culture to a leisure culture.

Many new industrial parks and apartments include tennis and volleyball courts, saunas and swimming pools to lure prospective tenants and businesses. My brother recently built a suburban office complex which is completely surrounded by a golf course, which, in turn, is surrounded by beautiful townhouse apartments. Again, expectations rise.

Women have been greatly affected by this shift in priorities in which self-worth and identity have become increasingly important. A woman's identity is no longer tied exclusively to a man's. Her culturally assigned role is no longer restricted to the home and raising children.

Marriage is no longer a security blanket but a means by which a man and a woman develop a close, loving relationship that is mutually satisfying to both of them.

Now, women find their worth in an ever-increasing variety of ways. All the work-saving devices recently introduced in the home have helped to create a sense of inadequacy in what was once a much-needed female role. Women in the home with blenders, frost-free refrigerators, frozen foods, automatic washers and dryers, dishwashers and garbage disposals suddenly find themselves with less to do, and the results can be devastating—loneliness and boredom. Alone with all the gadgets and conveniences of modern life, modern women quickly conclude there is more to life than watching TV and pushing buttons. They look for a more meaningful, involved life, for a way to be fulfilled in this newly developed free time.

The two elements—free time and work—will become more interrelated in the future. What to do in our leisure time is now the question. Excessive consumption of alcohol and hours of TV-viewing serve only to move persons further and further from their friends. Such activities are, in essence, self-defeating and will result in loneliness. The ultimate antidote for loneliness must be found in mutual, relevant involvement.

For those searching today, it is not just how much money they earn that makes them happy. It is what they do and with whom they do it that makes them feel good.

Thus, it is how you live your life, in terms of what you do with the time you have that ultimately determines whether you are happy or lonely. We all have twenty-four hours in a day. Think about it. Better yet, do something you enjoy and do it with others. See for yourself.

Write down your income and expenditures during the next month. List your expenses in order of their importance to you. How you use money can make your time more flexible and enjoyable. Look at the money available in your budget; can you channel more into recreation or leisure pursuits? For instance, a person may desire an expensive car but not have enough money left for his free-time desires such as sailing or traveling.

This was the case with Bill, a soft-spoken teen-ager. He had been working in the steel mill for a year, had saved his money, was single, and was thinking about buying an eight-thousand-dollar automobile. During a counseling session, he mentioned that he was disappointed because he wanted to take a trip out West to visit a close friend who had moved to Arizona but that he could not afford it. Later in the same session, he mentioned that he had gone sailing recently and would like to get a boat but could not afford it. Money seemed to limit what he wanted to do.

It had not occurred to him that he could buy a less expensive car and have enough left to take a vacation and still get the boat. The decision Bill had to make was one of priorities. Expensive car and no vacation? Less expensive car and vacation? Smaller car, vacation, and sailboat?

Think about how to cut your budget. Some examples might be:

Food: buy lower-priced meats
Car: used instead of new, or one that gets better gas mileage.
Apartment vs. house: how much should be spent
Furniture: is it really necessary, used or new
Appliances: used or new

Next, look at how you spend your time. Pick an average day in your life (see Figure 17). Take tomorrow, for instance, or keep track of how you spend your time every day for the next week. That is even better because the longer period of time enables you to get more perspective into how you typically spend your time. Look especially at two possibilities; increasing the time you can talk to or do something with another person and increasing the enjoyment and relevance in what you are actually doing.

	The Way I Spend My Time	Alternatives
7:00	Get up, have breakfast	Get up, have breakfast
8:00	Leave for work	Leave for work in a car pool or share ride
8:30	Arrive at work, go over morning reports	Go over morning reports, talk to secretary, fellow workers, boss, etc.
10:00	Coffee break in my office	Coffee break with others, start a little discussion group
10:20	Planning conference time	
11:00	Dictate letters, call customers	Stop and talk for five minutes with someone you seldom talk with
12:00	Lunch at corner restaurant	Take customer to lunch or go with fellow employee
1:00	Sales meeting	
2:00	Call on customers	Stop and talk for five minutes with someone you seldom talk with
5:00	Drive home	Drive home in car pool
6:00	Dinner alone	Dinner with friends; invite someone over
7:00	Do laundry and other things around apartment	
		Do something creative e.g. art work
8:00	Watch TV	Play Scrabble with a friend
9:00		Go bowling in a league and then go out for something to eat, or
10:00		Call parent or friend you seldom see
11:00	Watch late news	Read a book or Magazine
		Exercise or work a puzzle
11:30	Go to bed	Go to bed

Figure 17

As you look at how you spend your uncommitted time, keep in mind how you are spending your income. Ask yourself what things you can do to feel more satisfied, always remembering that people need people, for only in the warmth of human life and companionship can people find true happiness. How you spend your time and money can sometimes make the difference.

Chapter seven

Talking with a lonely person

Suppose you are lonely and in the hospital with no visitors. Talking with someone always seems to help. When a person becomes extremely lonely, he grows desperate to talk to someone, anyone. That is why help hot-lines and volunteer visitors have been so successful in many cities.

What many people do not realize is that you have to do more than just talk to a lonely person if you are really going to help. You have to know what to talk about and what to avoid. If all you do is to talk aimlessly, then you are just offering temporary relief. Unless you help make some plans to change their life patterns, nothing has been achieved. You have shared time and shown compassion. That is all.

Not that there is anything wrong with compassion. Every once in a while we all need a good listening post, and many times there is value in listening, especially as you build involvement initially. Some people cannot cope with plans for change right away, so for a while you talk about the weather or something unconnected with what is troubling them.

But just talking over our troubles is an improvement only if we compare it to not talking at all. Think of it like this. Let's say you have a severe headache from your job, and you take an aspirin. The aspirin is only temporary relief; what you really need is to change what you are doing on the job, or maybe to get a different job.

The fact that someone takes the time to listen to you does help; but after a while, if you continue to live your life as you always have, the headache will return. In other words, you talk a lot but do not change what you are doing; thus you do not solve much. So you go from person to person, friend to friend, telling them about your problem. You go from one listening post to another.

Lending someone an ear is sometimes called supportive therapy. Sometimes it does help you to see your situation more clearly, because it brings what you are doing out into the open where you can make some accurate value judgments. "Let's talk about it" is a good suggestion, for as the two of you talk it over, you feel closer. You have a friend.

You just have to remember that talk gives little permanent relief. Most problems are solved by action, not by talk. Sooner or later, when the talk is over and the sympathetic friend is gone, you have to get on with living your life enjoyably and effectively. Talking does give you the illusion that problems are being solved, but that is all it is—an illusion. If you do not come up with a specific suggestion or plan of action, no progress has been made.

When Elizabeth, a twenty-seven year-old mother of two children, first came in, she asked me where I wanted her to begin. She thought that beginning with her childhood experiences some twenty years ago would be a good place to start. Before I could reply, she asked if going back seven years, when she was turning down all those offers of marriage, would be good enough. I told her that just talking about yesterday would probably be good enough to show what she was doing with her life.

This came as quite a shock to Elizabeth. She said that all of her friends had listened to her talk about her past experiences. Many times she had started with her graduation from high school. In fact, she said she had relived almost every moment of the past twenty years when she talked with her next-door neighbor, Jo Ellen.

I said, "Did it help?"

"Well, I guess not. Nothing's changed," she said, "but Jo Ellen is so sympathetic."

"Did the sympathy make you feel better?"

"For a while." Elizabeth replied. "Every time I talk to her I feel better for an hour or two."

"Then what happens?"

"I begin to feel bad again."

"That's just the point. Talking about your past miseries and present troubles won't help you nearly as much as talking about what you can actually do to make things better."

Elizabeth then replied, "That would certainly cut down on my conversations. Don't you know that when we get together we spend hours discussing our problems?"

"Well, some women do and some women don't," I said. "And for that matter, a lot of men do the same thing, but it really doesn't change anything."

There are five things a person should not do when talking with someone who is lonely.

First, don't try to find out "why" people do things.

Many people spend hours and hours trying to learn why they do things. They are under the illusion that if they find out why they do things, they will solve their problems. Some call this insight, but there are many people who have a tremendous amount of insight and who still have the same problems. It is like the man who said, "I know why I gamble. I've always known, but I still do it."

People like to analyze why their friends do things because it's safe. It does not threaten anyone, and you can spend hours and hours in the analyzing stage without getting to the real hub of the problem. Some people will say, "Well, at least I understand why he does that." But understanding by itself does not help. You can have all the understanding in the world, and it will not change anything unless the person involved decides to do something about his own actions.

A fifty-five-year-old civil engineer once said to me, "I've been to six counselors. I know why I steal from stores. I understand why I am this way. But I can't seem to change. I've come to you for help. Can you help me?"

He had lots of understanding. He was bright. He was an engineer and could figure out almost anything. We did not spend any time on his past or why he was stealing. The basic question was: "Do you want to stop stealing?" If he answered yes, then we would go on from there. This is a very simple method of dealing with life's problems, and it is also very effective.

There is an inherent danger in discussing in too much detail why people do things. Once you think you know why someone does something, it is all too easy to accept that reason as an excuse for his behavior. It becomes too easy to label him and then forget about him. You have seen this happen many times. Someone says, "Poor Fred, he's an alcoholic, you know," and so we do not expect Fred to control his drinking. We make excuses for him: "Fred drinks because he lost his wife."

Second, don't talk about the past.

Maybe your friend's name is Norma, and she calls one night. She says she is depressed. She says she cannot seem to do anything right anymore. She starts talking about how no one in her family has ever been successful. She starts to cry. She says she is no good, like the rest of her family. You find out she has just failed a test to become a beautician.

Now you know the reason. You can discuss all the parts of the test and the reasons why she flunked the exam, and maybe that will show your sympathy; but if you do not get around to helping her see what she can do to retake and pass the test, you are remiss. Talk about something over which she has *some control and which she can do*. That is solid, helpful conversation which could bring results.

As far as discussing the inadequacies of her relatives is concerned, diplomatically point out that she is not responsible for what others do—only for herself. This entire line of reasoning where a person talks about family failures is an excuse for that person to lead an irresponsible life in the present. Just because your mother beat you when you were ten years old is no excuse for arguing and yelling at your own children today.

Third, don't try to find out whose fault it is.

Pat, a widower in his 70s, would say over and over, "My kids never come to see me. It's their fault I'm so lonely. They're the ones to blame. They don't appreciate all I've done for them over the years. If they did, they wouldn't treat me this way."

Maybe Pat was right. But finding out whose fault it was that he was lonely would not change anything. All it did was absolve him from the responsibility of doing something himself. We looked at what he could do himself. In two weeks, Pat was spending three afternoons a week at the Society for the Blind as a volunteer driver. He enjoyed this, and it did wonders for his self-image.

Judy and Jack, a teenage couple newly married, told me that, whenever they would have a disagreement, they would go over the entire incident and all the events leading up to it. That way they could find out whose fault it was. Their last spat was over who was to blame for not putting gas in the car. She said, "It's your fault, Jack. You forgot to have the car filled up with gas."

Jack said, "You drove the car last. I told you to check the gas gauge before we left."

"I thought you filled it up," she said. And on and on they would argue.

Judy said once they had spent a whole Saturday afternoon discussing and rehashing the events of a preceding evening just so they could find out who was to blame for the lousy evening they had.

I suggested they try something different. "Has arguing over who was at fault helped," I asked. "No," they replied. "Then stop arguing and do something you both enjoy together. If you discuss who's at fault, it will only cause more bad feelings between you. It won't solve anything."

Fourth, don't wallow in a person's feelings.

It is better to work with a lonely person on something which will help them do something better than to spend time commiserating or crying. If you hear a fire alarm, you act. You do not say, "I wonder why that alarm is ringing? It sounds awfully loud, doesn't it?" Or "Let's analyze why it rings." Like feelings, the fire alarm tells you something is wrong. Discussing the signal does little good.

People love to talk about how they feel, whether good or bad. If a person is lonely, he often clings to his bad feelings because they are all he has. His depression becomes his constant friend who will never leave him. If you get involved in his bad feelings, he will use these feelings as an excuse for not doing anything. If you suggest he do something, he will say, "When I feel better," or, "I don't feel like it."

The next time one of your friends tells you that they are depressed, try saying "What are you doing to make yourself depressed?" Now, what you are saying is, "I believe you're not happy. I accept that." But you are also saying, "Let's take a look at what you are doing that is causing the depression and figure out something better."

An attractive young college girl once came in saying she could not study because she was too nervous. After a long, friendly chat, I asked her if she really wanted to get through school.

She said, "Yes, I do." I replied, "Then somehow you will have to learn how to study with a nervous stomach. Many people get through college with worse ailments. They just figure out ways to cope with the problems they've got. If you can't study, you can't get through college. Let's figure out what you can do."

We reduced the number of classes she was taking to a more manageable number. Once she made up her mind she had to study, nerves or no nerves, stomach or no stomach, she began to study a half-hour each day. As she began to succeed at this small plan, she increased the study time.

Most people try to cheer people up by suggesting too many things for them to do. This was the case with Jill, a thirty-year-old teacher who came in asking what she could do to help a friend of hers. This friend had told her that she was so unhappy and depressed that she did not even get out of the house any more. Her friend would just sit around, smoke cigarettes, drink coffee, watch TV, and lounge around in a housecoat all day. Jill said that her friend was too depressed even to get dressed and that she had not had her hair done for months.

Jill told me how her friend would say, "I look so awful. I'm too embarassed to go to the beauty parlor with my hair looking like this." Then she would add, "Some day I'll do something with my hair; then when I look a little better, I'll call the beauty parlor for an appointment. After that, Jill, maybe we can have lunch together sometime." If you are determined to lose, you can't win, can you?

Jill asked what she could suggest to her friend who was housebound and depressed. She had already suggested that the woman get a job, get out of the house on weekends, call her friends more often, buy some new clothes, get the "works" at the local health spa, and then get a "full treatment" at a nearby beauty academy. "I know that would make her feel better," Jill said.

We would probably all agree that any or all of those things would make her friend feel better, but this is the typical kind of plan offered by one friend to another. It is well intentioned but too gigantic. It overwhelms the person who is miserable. Jill's friend, who couldn't even get herself out of her housecoat, was being asked to get a job, get out of the house on weekends, and so on. It is much easier to help people when you get them to take one step at a time. To ask them to take five or ten steps, when they are not sure about the first step, is too threatening. Remember, you feel good and they feel bad. What seems easy to you is awesome to them.

Fifth, don't waste time worrying about factors beyond the person's control.

A teenage boy who was not doing well in school said, "I can't pass the course because the instructor is so dry and dull."

"Do you want to pass the course?" I asked.

"Yes," was his answer.

"Then you have to figure out how to pass a course that has a dull and dry instructor," I replied.

"But let me tell you what he does," he said.

"Do you want to pass the course? You only have control over what you do, not what the instructor does."

Maybe you are talking with a person who has an obnoxious co-worker. Ask him, "Do you want to continue working at that job?" If the answer is "yes," then he has to figure out how to get along with the obnoxious person.

"But you don't understand, I can't even do my work when he's around. I can't stand him."

"Well, you have a choice. Learn how to live with him, get a transfer, or quit."

Everyone loves to use others as an excuse for their inability to live their lives more effectively. A man once came in with a drinking problem. He said, "Let me tell you about my problem. It's her." (His wife came with him.) "Everytime she starts nagging, I have to get drunk."

It is amazing how often we use others as an excuse for what we do. We say there are people who can drive us to drink; but in reality, *we* make the decision to drink, not the other people. We are responsible for ourselves. And we have to work at building our life *within the reality of our own situation.*

Remember, a person who comes to you asking for help has not been able to solve the problem on his own. He is asking, "What do you have to offer? What can you suggest that is better than what I have already tried?"

Finding out the reasons why people are upset will not change things. Pinning the blame on someone does not make anyone's life more tolerable. Get your friend to talk about what he is doing and *what he can do.* That is the real key to helping a lonely person overcome loneliness.

Chapter eight

Single, married, and. . .

Should I get married? Should I stay single? What about a divorce? Most people ask questions like these at one time or another. What they really want to know is what kind of life-style will give them the greatest happiness over the longest period of time. Although this is a matter of individual choice, most people have chosen to find this happiness through marriage—the most intimate form of interpersonal relationship man has ever known.

There has been a great deal of skepticism recently about the lasting quality of marriage, especially in light of the climbing divorce rate. Many young people openly express sarcasm about married life. Why get married? Marriage just for the sake of getting married is obviously the poorest excuse. But more than this, they see some married couples fighting, while others are not talking to each other at all. One young man said recently that so many of his buddies at work complained about their marriages that he was never going to get married. He told me, "It seems they got along fine before they were married; but once the knot was tied, all they have is misery and more misery."

Young people see good marriages, too. Many are products of happy families themselves, but the spiraling divorce rate concerns them. They look at divorce as an indication of failure. In our competitive, success-oriented society, nobody wants to fail. It is no wonder that many young people approach marriage with uncertainty and apprehension.

It takes more than sexual desire to sustain a marriage. Desire may be a great place to begin, but it is knowing how and what to do in a close personal relationship that makes it last.

Also, single life has many benefits: mobility, flexibility in career choice, and leisure-time activity. There is usually less stress involving a partner because single people do not have to work at getting along with another person as much as married people do. Many singles have close involvements with others, but they are ordinarily not locked into these relationships as they would be in marriage.

Also, single women often see marriage as a limit to their own development and growth, especially when a husband gets a promotion or transfer to another city. Why should they leave and start all over again? Many married men are deferring upward movement in favor of increased stability, higher quality of family life, or completion of a wife's academic endeavors or maintenance in a job she enjoys.

Whether you are single, married, or divorced does not matter. How you live your life is what counts. If you want to enjoy life, you should be around people who care about you. Otherwise, you not only feel lonely, you begin to feel that you do not count in the world.

One aspect of living alone which can lead to loneliness is the opportunity to become self-centered rather than other-centered. A single person does not have to think about others as much as a married person, especially one with children. If you do not have to think about others, your thoughts easily dwell on yourself. The result can be loneliness.

When you commit yourself to a more permanent relationship, such as marriage, you have more occasions for self-development because of your increased interpersonal responsibilities. The more commitments you make, the more effective your life. The people who undertake challenge and risk are the people who grow. Those who constantly avoid commitment usually live for the moment. They are always searching but never finding anything that lasts. Happy people are able to make deeper commitments and work longer to achieve their goals.

The degree of commitment you are able to make is a sign of your internal strength. You grow when you successfully handle the challenges life offers. Keeping your head above water when adversity hits you takes stamina and courage.

Weighty obligations and responsibilities can be frustrating; but conquering them can be well worth the frustration. Accomplishment always feels good. You cannot succeed at everything, but sometimes the fun is in the trying, even when there are temporary setbacks. You just replan and try something different.

Unfortunately, no one can adequately describe what a happy marriage is. Nor can anyone say what a satisfying single life is like. People can tell you about it, but you have to experience it yourself to really understand it. And what is best for one person might not be best for another. There is no one ideal way to live for all people.

The skills involved in interpersonal relationships are learned and developed as we grow up. At each stage in our growth, more is demanded of us in terms of our ability to get along with others. We tolerate much more abuse from children than we do from adults. When it comes to adults, we assume they know better.

There is no such thing as a totally independent person. To grow psychologically as human beings, we need people all of our lives. The most independent person is a catatonic in the back ward of a mental hospital.

As children, we *depend* on others for their love in order *to learn how to love*. As we move into our teens, we begin to develop the skills of loving by working at getting along with others. The skills of making and maintaining a relationship is something we work at all our lives. The older we grow, the more is demanded of us in terms of stress in relationships. Thus, the more we have to work at loving, the more we grow, and the more we can handle.

But we need others ultimately as someone to love. As I work at trying to get along with my wife, it is I who grow close to her. I love her for my own sake, not for hers. This is the paradox of love. For her to be happy with me, she has to work at getting along with me. The same is true with my children and my friends.

With less dependency, there will obviously be less involvement. With less involvement, less growth as a person. Also with less involvement, there is greater danger that a person or a relationship will not be strong enough to endure the stress of everyday living.

A person learns gradually about relationships in five stages, as shown in Figure 18. The age brackets shown next to each stage are just approximate.

As you can see, not everything is learned in childhood and merely put on instant replay later. It is not like the saying about not being able to teach an old dog new tricks. Certainly you can. It just takes a little longer, that is all. In relationships, as we grow older, it sometimes takes a little longer to achieve the relational balance we desire or are comfortable with.

"Advice to the lovelorn" columns frequently used to counsel men and women to "stay married at all costs for the children's sake." This is rapidly changing. Children are better off living with one happy parent than living in homes where the parents are locked in bitter conflict all the time.

RELATIONAL SKILLS DEVELOPMENT

Birth - 12 (child)	Dependence on parents for learning about love. Minor stress in some relationships with playmates such as learning to share, get along, etc. Imitation of how parents behave toward one another as well as others who are close, such as teachers.
13 - 19 (teenager)	Expansion of relationships with peers on the basis of what has been learned from parents and others. Attempts in early teens at relationships with the same, and then later, with the opposite sex but usually without a commitment. Tests of skills learned through earlier modeling of adults. If there is any stress, you separate and go home. In late teens, first attempts at close personal relationships with the opposite sex with some degree of commitment.
20 - 25 (young adult)	Further growth in relational development through marriage. You learn to get along with another under stress instead of separating and going home as in the teenager stage.
26 - 45 (adult)	Further growth in relational development as you work hard at getting along with your children, who do not necessarily work as hard at getting along with you. Usually growth in relational development at work as you try to get along with co-workers and also, those with whom you socialize.
46 + (mature adult)	The great age of sociability where social interaction shifts from family-and child-centered to a broader circle of friends. As children leave home, it is necessary to have a strong, close relationship with marriage partner and/or others to handle stress of loss of children. Deeper relational fulfillment and continued relational growth as children and grandchildren return.

Figure 18

Of course, the divorced parent faces many problems not found in a two-parent family. The single parent has to assume total responsibility for bringing up the children. There are often major changes in the economic condition of the family at this time, too. If the mother has not been earning an income, she is faced with the choice of living on alimony and child support payments or of going to work.

Reverting from married to single also means a change in the sex life of the single parent, and society has long held more restrictive sexual attitudes toward the single parent than toward a single person with no children. There are many people who unfairly look down on divorced persons as unstable or as failures. A formerly respectable married woman suddenly becomes viewed by some wives as a "threatening, promiscuous female." A formerly respectable, hardworking married man suddenly becomes some kind of sex maniac on the prowl.

Persons who decide to stay single often unjustly become categorized by some members of society as eccentric, old maids, bachelors, or swingers. When these people were young and single, they were deemed to be carefree and really able to enjoy themselves. It is only when people stay single too long that they become suspect to a society made up predominantly of married people. It is unfortunate that many still label people and look for stereotypes to verify their character images. Why not accept single people as individuals who have chosen a life that appeals to them?

Many single parents join clubs such as Solo Parents or Parents without Partners. These clubs provide a good opportunity for single parents to meet other people of the same age with similar interests. They are excellent channels for overcoming isolation, depression, and loneliness. They are fun, too. Members do things together like skiing or bowling and form friendships—at a time when friends are really needed.

These single groups also provide a good means for divorced people to overcome some of their own personal frustrations. Discussing some immediate problems and learning how others solved similar problems are helpful to a person going through the pain and trauma of separation and divorce. Breaking up is always hard, and a little support during this temporary crisis is very helpful. There is a therapeutic value in people helping each other adjust to a new way of life.

Becoming single after having been married is quite often a lonely life. Divorced people often say they want to marry again as soon as they find someone else. A few have even said they might remarry the same person. One woman said, "At least he was somebody to talk to. We did have some good times together. Now there's nobody."

A major problem facing single parents today is child care. Many young mothers find that inexpensive day-care facilities for their young children are inadequate, if not totally nonexistent. One mother said, "After I pay a baby-sitter every two weeks, there's not much left. Besides, it's really not good for the kids. I know it must be difficult for them to see their mother go off to work every day, especially when they don't have a father. My mother can't watch them. She works, too. And my ex-husband is unemployed, so the court reduced his payments for child support. What am I supposed to do? I don't like things this way. They're not the best, but I still think things are better now than when we were together and fighting all the time."

In spite of such obstacles, many people get divorced and raise their children successfully. Many single women who become pregnant decide to keep their babies and bring them up themselves. Often they continue to live at home, and their parents, usually shocked and dismayed at first, sooner or later become supportive and even get to be doting grandparents.

One day a twenty-two-year-old, career-bound mother said there was not much of a thrill in getting a promotion at work because half the fun was in sharing the joy with someone you love. "You come home and there's no one there." She said, "I could tell my baby, but that's silly. He's only six months old. Besides, you don't discuss things like that with your kids. It's just not the same. So that part of my life is still lonely. But I'm working on it," she added.

Young single mothers often say they think both a mother and a father are important in raising a child. But they quickly point out that their children are better off with them in a stable home environment than they were in a situation that was constantly upset.

"There's no doubt that little kids are better off when they have parents who are getting along," a divorced father said. "But I also think kids are better off with one happy parent than with two unhappy ones. If all they see is mom and dad arguing, that's hard on everybody. The kids lose out, as well as the parents. Nobody's happy."

A frustration often expressed by young divorced women with children is that they find it harder to get involved with available men. When they are out and they see signs of a possible intimate relationship developing, it is often "time for them to go home and take care of the kids because the baby-sitter has to get home early." More than one young divorced woman has told me, "When a man finds out you already have kids at home, he'll dump you. I don't blame them, though. Who wants to raise somebody else's kids?"

It is often harder to start a romantic relationship with a new partner when you have other responsibilities that limit you, such as the obligations of raising children or making child support payments. This is true for both men and women. They all say that the more children you have by a previous marriage, the harder it is to find someone who is willing to get serious or get married.

An unforgettable client was a young woman in her late twenties who was sobbing because her husband had suddenly told her he was going to leave her and their three small children. Amidst her tears she said, "I'll never find anyone else."

We talked for a while that first day Marla came in and made some plans about what she could do to put her life back together. She said, "I guess you're right. Life goes on anyway." We started by working on getting her a job.

For a few weeks, nothing seemed to go right. Then one afternoon a department store called and asked her to start the following Monday. She met a lot of new friends and started to go out again. Marla began to date a few of the men she would meet at work. One day when she was in a hurry to get home because her mother was baby-sitting for her an attractive man in his mid-twenties walked over and asked her where to find a particular item. They talked for a few minutes, and he asked if she would go out to get something to eat after she finished work. Marla wanted to, but she said she had to get home and take care of her children. Without batting an eye, he said, "Fine, I'll take you home." Marla was a little hesitant and skeptical at first, but after a little coaxing finally agreed. They stopped for a quick cup of coffee on the way home. The next evening they went to a show, then out to eat. It was not long before they were dating.

Joe said that Marla's three kids just "gave them a head start." The children liked Joe, and that relieved a lot of anxiety for Marla, who was worried about how the children would react to a new man who was going to be their father. It was not long before Marla and Joe got married. I ran into them by accident one night in the line waiting to go into the theater. I looked ahead and there were Joe, Marla and the children. They were doing fine.

It can be just as hard for a man to be a single parent as it is for a woman. A divorced father wants to see his children (if the children have remained with the mother) and get close to them, but that is not always easy. After a while he usually runs out of places to take them on the days they are with him. He does not like to take them to his place, and yet he is supposed to keep them all day. What do you do after you have gone bowling every other Sunday for six months, tried every ice-cream parlor in town, and been on all the rides in the local amusement park at least five times for the past six Sundays in a row? How many times can you go to the zoo during a three-month period?

That is not all that faces a divorced father. What about trying to meet alimony or child-support payments while trying to pay the installments on the car he bought to boost his sagging, damaged ego when his ex-wife started dating his best friend? What about those long cold lonely nights? What about the choice he faces between spending his day off in the local laundromat or coping with the costs of skyrocketing laundry bills? How about all the blind dates his friends and relatives constantly fix him up with? And last but not least are those endless nights of TV dinners—some cold, some hot—all while watching the six o'clock news, alone.

One of the hardest things for any human being is coming home and knowing no one is there. That is when it really can get lonely. The hustle and bustle of the day is over and the tempo slows down. That is a relief. But the slowed pace may bring with it a momentary feeling of emptiness, which is further accentuated and complicated by feelings of loneliness. It is not that there are not enough things for a single person to do; it is that, at times, he or she would rather do them with another person.

For many, however, the time after work is a much desired time for some creative activity apart from the noisy and busy world. The point is to find a balance between the time you want to be alone and when you want to be with others. This varies with each person.

The bustle of a busy office full of people could lead a person to the joy of an interesting, thoughtful activity alone in his or her own apartment. To another, a lonely, noninvolving job might develop the desire for more human involvement later in the day. Some require companionship most of their waking hours while others require very little to satisfy this basic relational need.

Despite all the ferment and change, all the ups and downs, despite all you read about the drawbacks of married life, marriage is more popular than ever. More than nine out of every ten Americans will marry at some time in their lives. The remarriage rates for those who do get divorced or widowed are also extremely high. Regardless of the fact that many marriages end in divorce and many couples have difficulties in getting along, marriage still remains a dominant, sought-after goal for almost everyone in our country.

Misconceptions of what marriage is or ought to be are everywhere. Marriage does not have to mean that one partner dominates the other. Marriage does not mean being subservient to each other's whims and wishes. It should not be an arrangement where people constantly take turns leaning on each other for the sake of keeping the marriage together. And it does not mean that both people live independently of each other and view life as two separate journeys, never to be shared. Marriage is not a lifetime trap that locks you into or out of anything, and it is not something to be reviewed weekly, like the office football pool, to see if you win or lose, or if you still want to play.

Marriage is what you make it, and that is no cliche. There are many meanings attached to the word "marriage." And there are many variations in what marriage turns out to be. Figure 19 shows three distinct views of married life.

How you live your marriage is, of course, your own choice. Each person chooses the way in which he or she feels most comfortable. However, it is important to be aware of the options, especially when considering whether to stay single, get married, or become single again.

OUTLOOKS ON LIFE

TRADITIONAL MARRIAGE	INDIVIDUALISTIC MARRIAGE	MARRIAGE AS SHARED LIFE
A series of problems to be conquered and solved.	Two individual and independent journeys through life.	Maturing relationship, strengthened as couple lives and shares life together. Not independent journey or a set of problems to be overcome, but a series of mysteries to be lived and enjoyed together.
Denial of self.	Personal growth.	Giving of self in order to find happiness with other.
Locked in forever, with no change in relationship.	Marriage commitment is subject to periodic, if not constant, review.	Review of what you can do to make things better.
Marriage above all else.	Individuals above marriage.	Emphasis on relationship and sharing.
Rigid role-expectations for male and female. A division of labor concept.	Reversal of roles, or roles independent of marriage.	Flexible; does not really matter who does what.
Nothing changes once it is established in the early days of the marriage.	Extremes. Constant change, nothing ever defined.	Not important who does it, but (1) it gets done, (2) they do it together.
SEX		
Absolute fidelity (at least for women, men are expected to be unfaithful).	Infidelity by both partners is sanctioned.	May be attracted to someone, but relationship and commitment are enough to make infidelity unnecessary.
LOVE		
No growth; static relationship tied to parternal and maternal responsibilities.	Growth occurs for the most part independently of the other.	Growth comes from working at relationship and in doing things together.
IDENTITY, GROWTH		
Subservient to marriage; partner identified as husband or wife, not as a person.	Comes from doing what you want.	Comes from (1) the development of the relationship and (2) doing things which you believe to be of value or worth.

Figure 19

	EACH OTHER	
Taken for granted.	Mixture of love and being taken for granted.	constant development of relationship and growth toward each other.
	TRUST	
Never questioned, expected and demanded.	Not required to any great degree.	Seen through what each does.
	CHILDREN	
Often taught to be carbon copies of parents. Focus on obedience.	Vulnerable to the tenuousness of the relationship; if the parent gets an urge to grow, the children may suffer.	The product and the object of love and concern; raised to be themselves with responsibility and success as a foundation.

Chapter nine

Living with another

A number of unmarried people live together for various reasons. There are many variations in these relationships, but many of their problems and joys are similar to those of marriage. However, living together does have its own set of unique difficulties.

Many times a person decides to live with someone because it is better than living alone. Whether for companionship, economy, or security, the fact remains that many persons like to live with someone else. It may or may not be with someone of the opposite sex; but whenever two people live together, they have to learn to get along.

Quite often living together is a platonic relationship with no sex involved; and other times the primary motivation in living together is sex. From college roommates, to senior citizens, to working persons, to homosexuals, to trial marriages, whether the two persons are the same sex or the opposite sex, if they share the same residence they want their relationship, whatever it is, to be enjoyable.

There are many advantages to living with another person: companionship, the possibility of loving someone more intimately, the security of having someone else around, economy, the chance to share with someone more directly what you do, the availability of help when sickness or death occur. With the variety of motives for living together, one might expect a variety of problems. However, I have observed the opposite—there are some definite commonalities found in all interpersonal problems. People are always people; we all have the same kind of nervous system, and the techniques of relating humanly are much the same for everyone.

Whenever human beings decide to live together, there is always more stress. Stress comes because no two people do everything exactly alike, and the attempt to adjust to another's actions always proves difficult. The closer you live, the greater the need to adjust. It is foolish to expect two people to agree on everything. It would be a pretty dull life if they did.

If the relationship is a good one, the joys will far outweigh the disadvantages. People have a basic need to be with people. It is certainly more fun to share and enjoy your interests with another person. No one wants to be lonely, and the desire to live with another is as basic as breathing. This is not to say that living alone is not desirable; it is just that most prefer to live with another.

It is this kind of thinking that prompts some people to decide to try living together for a while. Yet if people can move apart easily whenever there is any stress imposed on their relationship, or if they can simply call it quits whenever they disagree, then their chances of building a lasting relationship are immeasurably reduced from the very outset. They must be willing to accept the responsibility for working at the relationship by making a stronger, more lasting commitment to each other. This is what it takes to make a relationship endure and grow through all the ups and downs that life offers when two people live together for any sustained length of time. That is the maturing process. Living with another, if there is to be a good relationship, requires a great deal of effort on the part of both. Without such effort, we remain perpetual children.

When a couple is dating and has a little squabble, they both know they can go their separate ways later. However, once married, they suddenly find themselves working much harder to make their relationship work. Some say this whole thing is like a trap. I don't agree. I believe it is the deep commitment between two people who care about each other that is so important. They are willing to accept the responsibility to work at the relationship instead of giving up when they run into stress and problems, and the relationship begins to drift. This is an extremely important distinction between married people and two people who take up a common residence. The degree of commitment two people bring to a relationship is the vital factor.

It is almost impossible for single people living together to develop as much of a commitment to each other as two people who are married to each other. One reason is that there is no external commitment. Another reason is that time helps build commitment between two people, and single people living together usually do not live together long enough to experience this growth. Some contend that, whenever two people live together, there must be a certain degree of commitment. This may be true, but it is *less of a commitment* than that made between two people who take a vow to work at the relationship in "good times and in bad." The chances that the love between these two will grow stronger is much greater as they spend more and more of their lives together over a longer and longer period of time.

If two people who are living together have a disagreement or a fight, they have to learn to handle the difficulty while continuing to live together the same as a married couple. Often this is too much for them to handle. This is one of the keys to understanding why some relationships fail so miserably in such a short time. For any close, meaningful relationship to last, it must have relational strength, which takes *time and effort* to develop. You develop this through what you do together, through working at getting along with another. Whenever two people work at getting along, the relationship grows stronger.

It is important for a person to build strength and confidence in himself so he can handle the rigors of everyday life. It is equally important to build strength and confidence into your relationship with another human being for some of these very same reasons. This strength or bond also helps two people to get more out of the moments they share together. It makes the good times better and the bad times bearable. Any relationship becomes better when both people work at it.

If only one person puts forth most or all of the effort, the relationship will fail. A major effort by both means a better chance at a happier relationship. If one person is exerting ninety percent of the effort and the other ten percent, there is little hope. Rarely do both work equally as hard. The person with the most to lose generally works the hardest.

Whatever the reason people give for the way they lead their lives, it is interesting to note that more and more people are beginning to recognize that making a binding commitment means there is a greater chance that the relationship will last. The relationship benefits from the higher sense of personal commitment. Perhaps some evidence of what I am saying here can be seen in the recent attempts of homosexuals to marry within the legal framework of society rather than just live together as they have done in the past. At least part of the reason for their desire to be legally married is an effort to create a visible sign of a more binding commitment in which two people really have to work at their relationship. In other words, they are more committed to work at getting along with each other. Whenever two people know they have to get along, they do try harder.

The relationship between homosexuals has its difficulties. In many communities people will not tolerate those who live together as homosexuals. The lack of tolerance and acceptance, as well as the absence of any strong external commitment, all tend to make this way of living more difficult and tenuous. Also, the problem of job transfer or better opportunities in another area creates stress, especially if one of the persons wants to move and the other prefers to remain. Add to these disadvantages the natural stress that occurs in any relationship, and one sees that living together for homosexuals is not altogether easy. The great advantage, of course, is the opportunity of sharing mutual interests.

Almost any relationship can coast along when times are good, and there is no upset or trauma. It is when times get tough that the weak relationships break down. For example, if there are no problems in the apartment, plenty of food in the refrigerator, and you are enjoying an evening of pleasant music and good conversation plus a refreshing drink, it is not hard to get along. But if the toilet is plugged up, the dryer does not work, the refrigerator is empty, the rent is two months overdue, and your roommate has burned a hole in your favorite overstuffed chair, then you experience stress; the relationship is tested.

Furthermore, even when two people of the opposite sex live together in an unmarried situation, they sometimes come under a great deal of social pressure. A young woman accountant in her mid-twenties told me that she and her boy friend, with whom she was living, could handle their relationship, but their parents could not. "When we would go to either home, our parents would get upset and keep suggesting we get married. When relatives would come over, they would start throwing in a few digs and our folks would get more upset than ever. Also, at a family reunion, everyone tried to figure out the relationship between Nelson and me. A couple of times we tried being perfectly frank and saying right out that we were living together. But a lot of the people couldn't handle that. So we began to visit home less often."

Perhaps we should compare marriage and living together to the degree of permanency two people desire. The less desire there is for permanency in a relationship, the less commitment two people are willing to give to each other (either orally or in writing). Obviously, then, the more desire two people have for permanency, the more likely the two are to get married.

When two people decide to live together without getting married, they usually do so with less of a deep and lasting commitment than would two people when they marry. I believe that is the basic idea behind living together. People are not sure things will work, and they want to try for a while. There are exceptions, of course, but even when two people say that they are going to live together and that they are determined to make their relationship last, they both know that if things do not work out they can walk away from the relationship more easily than if they were married. This means their relationship is basically starting from a weaker vantage point than that of a married couple because married people ordinarily do not look at things the same way. Perhaps it is a state of mind, but two people who are newlyweds generally enter into the marital relationship feeling more confident about making it work and about their long-range future together. Two people who decide to live together are more confident about the immediate present and less confident about what the future holds.

Young people say to me, "Big deal. What does a marriage license mean?" I believe that whenever people will not sign things it is usually because they are uncertain about a lasting commitment or because they do not want to accept the responsibility for having to work at a relationship under stress. "What if I change my mind?" they usually ask. People have doubts about many things: themselves, their future, their job, their. . . who knows? Uncertainty about marriage scares some people.

Marriage is a long-term commitment to the unknown future that requires the effort of two people in order to succeed. Often one person is confident in his or her own ability to make a marital relationship work. They know they are willing to try, but they do not have enough confidence in the other person or in the relationship. They are not sure their partner will put forth enough effort so that the marriage will succeed. Marriage is like a team; it takes the effort of both partners to succeed. Consequently, even though some people may want to get married, they choose instead to remain alone or just live with another.

Commitments are a part of life. Almost every card you carry in your wallet, such as your driver's license, or credit cards, are valid only after you have signed them. Usually you have to sign an application form to get the card in the first place. To pursue this same point, look in a safe-deposit box. Insurance forms, mortgages, titles, licenses, vouchers, bonds—all important documents carry signatures. What is more, it seems that the more important the documents are, the more signatures they carry. A signature has long been accepted as visible evidence of a person's commitment. Most people think that if you do not have to sign for something in one way or another, it must not be worth much.

When it comes to relationships, how much are they worth? Are they worth signing for? Are they worth more than your car? An interesting effect of putting things in writing is that people always feel more obligated when they sign their name. Bankers and lawyers have realized this for years. Otherwise, why would they have you sign everything? Try telling them that your word is good enough, and see what happens. They might even say they believe you, but they still ask you to sign. Mysteriously, after you sign, you somehow feel more obligated. So it is with marriage. When you sign the papers to be married, you feel you have committed yourself as a responsible adult.

For some, living with another person of the opposite sex in an unmarried state can be a very serious matter. For others, it's taken very casually. Women have more to lose in this arrangement. First, the older a woman is, the harder it is for her to get married, if ultimately this is what she wants to do. While she is living with a man without commitment, her chances of a permanent marriage continually diminish. He can end the relationship and find another younger partner much more easily than she can. Second, the number of women who are available and interested in marriage outnumber men in this country. Thus a woman's chances of getting a commitment out of her partner are less because he already has her exclusively. He lives with her but without having to develop any responsibility for working at the relationship. You may say that a woman has the options, and this would be true if the numbers of men and women interested in marrriage were equal. But, the numbers are not equal, and since available and interested women do outnumber men, it is therefore more advantageous for a woman to have a meaningful commitment from a man before she lives with him.

If two people decide to live together, whether of the same or opposite sex, there are some basic factors to consider. A mutual understanding on some matters prior to moving in together can save a lot of heartache later.

Will one person do things in the apartment that the other person may strongly object to? What are their likes and dislikes? For instance, one couple I know lived together and got along fine for about six weeks, before they started having heated arguments over what kind of music was to be played in their apartment. After a while, it was not only a question of what kind of music was to be played but how long and how loud! She loved to play jazz music as loud as possible for hours on end. He said that kind of music really got on his nerves. They began to argue more and more. One thing led to another, and one day they exchanged some pretty harsh words. Later their arguments evolved into more physical means of settling things, but that really settled nothing—or maybe everything, depending on how you look at it. Because that settled their living together. They quit living together after that. So some understanding or idea of what the other person is like is helpful.

It is also helpful if the two people sharing the same residence approve of the same things. Pets, for instance. Do they both like dogs? Cats? Are there to be any animals? Who is going to take care of these pets? How about other interests or hobbies?

What about costs? What happens if one eats a lot and the other decides to go on a diet? Who pays the grocery bill then? Is everything to be divided equally on a cost basis regardless of who eats what? What about the utilities? Repairs? Maintenance? Who does what cleaning and how often? Who pays for incidentals?

What about having friends and relatives over? One young college girl told me she really got fed up with sharing a two-room apartment with another girl because, everytime she came home, her girl friend was in bed with a boy friend. She said she could cope with that once in a while, but on several occasions it had proved to be rather embarrassing, especially once when her mother came to visit.

Even if two people living together get along, sometimes others in the neighborhood cannot accept that life-style, especially if it is unique or unusual. It is a case of fitting into the community where you live. Some people say, "I'm going to live however I want to. Nobody pays my bills. I don't care what the neighbors think." The problem with this is the neighbors do think, and they do exert a certain amount of pressure, either seen or unseen, which can cause some uncomfortable feelings.

The unexpected can also occur when one partner suddenly changes his or her familiar habits or patterns. People do change, and they usually do not give you any warning. Suddenly your friend decides he likes to watch all-night movies even though you like to go to bed early. When people change they no longer do all the predictable little things they used to do. What happens when they say they are tired of paying the phone bill because they do not use the phone, or they are not going to help with the dishes anymore? No specific reason; they just do not feel like it. Then what? These unexpected changes can be troublesome. The balance of the relationship is upset temporarily, and it takes time for two people to readjust. If their relationship is unstable or weak in any way, the new adjustment might involve separation.

Cynthia and Luke, both medical technicians, thought it would be a good idea to live together for a while without getting married. They thought they might get married some day, but they could always decide that later. "At least it would cut expenses," Luke said. "We both had apartments, and that was foolish. Half the time we were either at her place or mine anyway." They leased an apartment and decided that all expenses were to be on an equal basis.

Things went along well for a while. They planned how the housekeeping jobs were to be divided. Then the craziest, most unsuspected thing caused them to start arguing—the windows. They started to argue, at length, about whose job it was to clean the windows in their apartment.

Such an argument may sound ridiculous, but this small, insignificant problem showed that their relationship, regardless of how strong it once was, was beginning to weaken and could no longer handle the normal stress which occurs when two people live together. A logical alternative for them might have been to do the windows together.

Their relationship was not strong enough to handle even this small amount of stress. Usually, physical harm and even murder are the result of very petty issues. Because separation was easier than accepting the responsibility of figuring out what they could do to build the relationship, they agreed to call it quits.

This is typical of many people. We tend to do the opposite of what we should do. When two people start to have difficulty, they begin to do less and less together, which is the opposite of what they should do. They should spend more time doing things together. They should do things to please and move closer toward the other. That would keep their relationship going.

In everyday life, we all face unexpected stress. When you live with someone, whether as friend or lover, things constantly change; people constantly change. Time never stands still, and no one ever stays the same. This is seldom a problem when two people both work at growing together and see life as worthwhile. Then the relationship between them continually develops. They change together.

When I last talked to Cynthia, she said she had learned something from living with Luke. She said next time she was going to put more effort into making things work out.

"If Luke and I had been married, I think we both would have worked harder at building our relationship. We argued about silly things, but we both knew we could call the whole thing off any time we wanted. In fact, toward the end, we often used to resort to that as our ultimate threat. After you've said, 'I'm leaving,' what else can you say?"

Chapter ten

Sex and loneliness

Many lonely people turn to sex to solve their problems. They think they can attract and/or hold onto someone if they offer them sex. But sex can be deceptive. It promises involvement but never delivers. During sexual intercourse, problems momentarily disappear; but as soon as sex is over, the pain of loneliness is back. Sex is only one aspect of life. It does not help in raising children or holding a job. *Sex has absolutely nothing to do with building the strength needed to handle the stresses in a close relationship.* Sex does, however, give increased enjoyment to an already strong and loving relationship. It is momentarily pleasurable, and nothing is missed so much as when it is absent; yet it occupies such a small amount of time in a person's total life span. The greatest thrill in sex is when you work to give your partner enjoyment. Your own pleasure then increases proportionately.

Sex is a natural part of any loving relationship, but it will not hold even a marriage together if the rest of the relationship is falling apart. Women have usually understood this better than men. That is why most women look for companionship and commitment from a man before becoming sexually involved. Men sometimes refuse to admit that sex does not overcome their loneliness or fulfill their need for love. Most women have sex with a person;

many men have sex for its own sake. They like to have "people-toys." These differing attitudes toward sex are crucial in understanding how a person can have sex and still be lonely.

A young female client of mine, recently divorced and very attractive, once said to me, "Aren't there any men around who like you just for yourself? Every man I go out with is all hands. All they do is grope and paw you to death. Can't they just be friends? All they want is sex, sex, and more sex. I'm tired of that whole scene, I've stopped going out. Now I sit home and feel so lonely that all I want to do is cry."

However, I have also had some lonely men come in and say "What's the matter with women? Every woman I go out with thinks I'm after her body. I just want to have a good time. I can get sex whenever I want it, but what I want is to go out and have a nice time. I want to enjoy myself and not think about whether or not we're going to bed later."

These two examples reflect our current mixed-up views about sex. The confusion is not surprising because we are constantly told that sex appeal is a crucial element in happiness.

Sex sometimes is used as a quick way to get intimately involved with another person. People who are lonely often think that having sex with someone is better than staying home alone. Sex always gives the illusion of caring. Having sex affords such powerful feelings that it is easy to believe that you are experiencing the feelings of true love and authentic involvement.

Sex gives some of the most intense feelings of pleasure that a human being can know. But the good feelings found in sex can be confusing, especially if a person is already suffering from rejection, despair, and loneliness. Words themselves are confusing because people say "Let's make love,'' when they mean, ''Let's have sex.'' Sex can be just sex or it can be another expression of an already existing love relationship. The most devastating experience for an already lonely person is to find that they have been ''used.'' In the eyes of the ''other'' they were not a person at all but a toy.

True love grows out of the relationship itself, not just from sexual attraction. Any time two people come together and are attracted to each other, the question of sex eventually arises. In order for two people to make a choice as to what is best for them, it would seem that sex should be looked at in terms of their entire relationship.

In short-term relationships, which are based primarily on ''speed'' (see chapter 4), there are intense feelings caused by the newness of the person as well as the sexual attraction. However, these feelings come and go very quickly. The pain of loneliness or separation in this type of short-term relationship is minimal and short-lived. High schools are full of ''tragic breakups'' one day and ''hot new romances'' the next. In searching for someone to love, it is easy to mistake the thrill of physical attraction for deeper and more meaningful involvement.

We all have a psychological need for love as well as a physical urge for sex. These are two absolutely distinct realities. The challenge is to meet these needs in a lasting, meaningful way in order to feel happy most of the time.

Animals seem to have instinctive controls for their physical needs. In their natural setting, for example, you rarely if ever see overweight animals. Unlike animals, man has to control his urges through decisions made by using his brain. He alone has to decide what is the best thing to do. Nature does not care about the ''speed'' found in a human relationship. All nature cares about is that people come together and have sex; it does not care whether they get together to raise children. Sex is strictly a biological urge.

Through various and complicated cultural practices, societies have set up all kinds of obstacles and barriers to the biological urge we refer to as the feeling of sex. Such procedures as courtship, chaperones, and family involvement have been built in to allow time for the couple to get to know each other better and to make a more rational, objective commitment to each other. These procedures are, in essence, attempts to place some rational restraints on our biological drives. The couple must learn to enjoy their relationship in aspects other than the sexual. In their wisdom, older men and women down through the centuries have tried to protect a young couple by customs so that the foundation of the couple's relationship is built on involvement along with a definite commitment. It is foolish to disregard these safeguards in the name of passion, love or haste.

Living together just for sex and then separating may sound ideal to those who like the Playboy philosophy. But this philosophy does not always work out in practice. Sex has a tendency to move people together with more rapidity than they are prepared to handle. People adjust to familiarity in a relationship rather slowly, as a rule. Familiarity brings stress. Sexual intercourse has an extreme amount of familiarity; and if it comes too fast in the development of the relationship, stress will follow. Stress that comes too early in a relationship, before strength is built, tends to leave the fragile, developing relationship open to destruction. Building relational strength takes time, lots of time. Sex itself actually accentuates loneliness *when there is no genuine love*. But if there has been love built into the relationship, then there are feelings of happiness and contentment. Familiarity in a fragile relationship without strength and caring, places a person in a highly vulnerable state.

The reason many close friends fight more after they decide to live together is that they often work at the relationship less and they experience more stress because they are living together more closely. All the secrets are gone. Familiarity is there.

There is a correlation between how much internal strength a person has and his or her ability to move slowly in a relationship. The stronger the person is, the more cautious he is about the sexual involvement. Why? Because he already feels pretty good about life and is not trying to use sex to blot out his bad feelings. He wants to avoid the pain that comes when new relationships become overextended and collapse.

When a relationship is first formed, there is no strength, only an illusion that somehow strength will be there when it is needed. Strength develops from what we do. The objective is to build sufficient strength in a relationship so that it can handle the stress and problems that will come along. Some relationships make it. Some do not. There are four stages in the development of a love relationship as outlined in Figure 20.

Some say free love is great, but free love is neither free nor is it love. It is not free because the term "free" implies receiving without giving something in return or without effort. Furthermore, it is not love because love implies the willingness to work constantly at a relationship. There is no effort or work in a sexual encounter.

Lonely people sometimes think they will be happier if they can improve their sex life. They think of sex as a means of overcoming boredom, depression, and loneliness. If sex with one partner does not make them feel good, they look for a new and different sexual partner in hopes they will solve their problem of loneliness.

If a person depends on sex to feel good, then the whole concept and place of sex in a relationship becomes

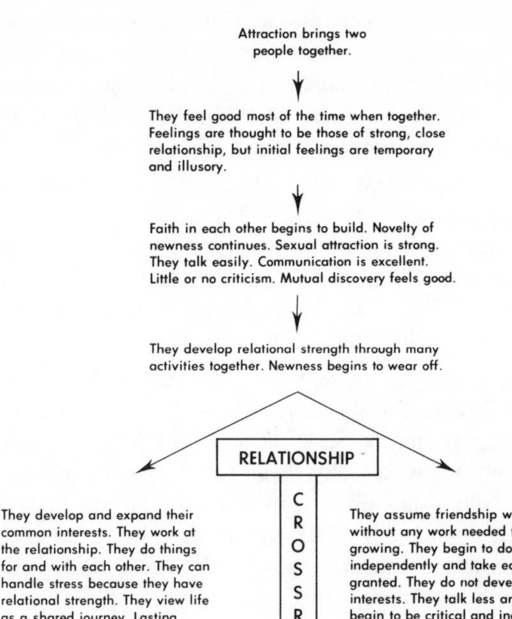

Figure 20

distorted. For instance, after you buy a new car and get over the initial thrill of ownership, and the new smell and the shiny look begin to diminish, then the car becomes just another car. The same is true with sex. Lasting enjoyment of sex with one person demands that you build a strong "depth" relationship with that person. Building involvement and doing things you both enjoy during the dating stage is highly desirable, if not essential. It helps the couple get along after the thrill of having each other sexually is over. As a counselor, I have never had anyone come to me and say, "I don't know how to have sex. How do you do it?" What usually happens is people come in and say, "How can we get along? We're fighting all the time, and our relationship is miserable."

Thus, it is not how do you have sex; it is how do you get along *after you have had sex?* This is one good reason why both the man and woman should withhold sex initially to see if they are willing to develop the commitment in the relationship. Then they know they like each other for themselves, not merely for sex.

A young woman came to me recently who was extremely depressed. She said she was thinking about committing suicide because she was so lonely. She said she had no one who really loved her in spite of frequent sexual relationships. She was having sex with half a dozen men each month. All it did was increase her feelings of loneliness and depression because she was not involved with people who really cared about her.

A lot of the advertising today promotes a false idea about sex. Cars are shown with sexy girls in mini-skirts, a blonde bombshell advertises the smoothness of new razor blades, and deodorant and toothpaste ads show intimate embraces with promises of instant popularity if you just clean and brush your teeth with fluoride. Male superstars are shown with women who use a certain brand of vitamins or hair rinse.

And now sex is marketed in an unending series of "how-to" manuals. Here, at last, is the answer to your problems—to loneliness. Some sex manuals try to help couples develop better ways to enjoy sex and to overcome sexual difficulties. For those who have problems in this regard, fine. But for people whose lives are empty, who use sex only as a means of filling the void in their lives, these books are about as much help as a refrigerator is for an Eskimo.

A high school girl who feels rejected, a working woman who is lonely and bored, a man who feels frustrated and trapped in his job—all these people may be fascinated by the possibility of using sex as a means of forgetting their unpleasant circumstances. But it compares to ordering a gourmet meal when you cannot pay the bill. The facade will quickly give way to reality. And that is where we live—in the world of reality.

If you think staying at home is painful, and sex is the price to go out, are you willing to pay the price? Often people choose to do things because it is less painful than doing something else. For example, you choose the pain found in a shot of Novocain from your dentist rather than suffer the pain of having a tooth filled without it. No one thinks Novocain feels good. It just feels "less painful." As Novocain reduces physical pain, so sex is sometimes used to reduce the mental pain of loneliness.

A young, pregnant, unwed mother came in one day. She said, "I thought he cared for me. That's why I let him make love to me. He said he loved me, and I believed him. We went together for almost a year before I became pregnant. Now I haven't seen him for six weeks. I've tried to call him, but he won't answer the phone. I was so lonely before I met him. I can't go back to the way things were before. I can't believe this whole thing is happening to me. I can't believe he doesn't love me. Now my life is so empty. I love him so much."

It is important for lonely people to understand that sex before commitment just makes real commitment much harder, if not impossible. Some young people say it is good to get sex out of the way early so that it does not play an all-important part in their relationship. They have a lot of sex without any commitment to each other. However, while they are having sex and doing some other things they enjoy together, it is easy for them to put off any commitment. "It will come with time," they reason. The problem is, it generally does not. Is the chance worth it?

Chapter eleven

Our lonely TV culture

Television is the great American escape. Since its introduction in the post-World War II years, TV has had an unbelievable impact on American life. Ninety-seven percent of all homes in this country have at least one set, and in the average household TV is on more than six hours daily. The average adult views TV in excess of five hours per day, and some studies conclude that preschool children watch TV more than eight hours daily. In many homes the set is turned on by the first person that gets up and turned off by the last person to go to bed.

TV occupies the eyes and ears of the viewer. With radio, a person can move around and do other things. Radio, unlike TV, does not occupy us totally, limiting our mobility. Actually, to some extent, radio stimulated the imagination. A person's mind created what radio lacked—a picture. Radio, unlike TV, required some active participation on the part of the listener.

Television by its nature does not foster creativity and social interaction. It is entertaining and educational. It fills time, but it does not fulfill a person's need for human contact and interaction. After the set is turned off, the pleasurable feelings also turn off.

The problem with passive activities such as TV is that they never last. Active pursuits like tennis, bowling, horseback riding, or boating give some involvement and a lasting sense of pleasure. The more you put in to something, the more you get out, including sustained good feelings and internal strength.

Heavy TV viewing is the favorite pastime for many lonely people. Studies have shown that extremely heavy viewers are most likely to have problems of social adjustment, to be more distracted in carrying on conversations with others, and to be more passive in interpersonal situations. But excessive TV viewing may be a symptom, not a cause, of the individual's retreat from social interaction.

It is certainly true that excessive TV watching does not encourage or help one to develop the ability to socially interact with others. Television creates an illusion of involvement for the viewer—an illusion that he is involved with others and that everything is all right. Television offers emotional stimulation without the risk of actual involvement. A housewife who watches a soap opera can become involved emotionally for the time that she watches. But she can turn off the melodrama whenever she wants, and she does not actually feel the pain of what the actors would be going through in real-life situations. Reality becomes distorted.

An artificial world is created in which people kill, rob, cry, laugh, or win thousands of dollars while not actually feeling the realities of life. The distinction between the real and the artificial becomes blurred. The viewer sees a world on TV and, after a while, feels that this is the real world. Sometimes it is good to get away from the demands of the world, but *excessive* watching distorts one's sense of reality. When the viewer can no longer distinguish between fantasy and reality, he begins to believe that the real world is a pushover—a place where only a little responsiblity and work are needed for success.

TV tells us we do not have to work at making friends or

being happy because a sweet-smelling soap will cause it to happen for us. Slug it out, but no one gets hurt. Laugh it up, but what is really so funny? The goal is distraction, to help us forget our troubles, but unfortunately our troubles will not go away while we sit there.

TV not only shows violence but teaches it. When a person has the sufficient strength to handle stress, seeing the violent and erratic behavior on TV has little effect upon him. However, to the weak and lonely, who have little strength when they meet stressful situations, violent programs on TV teach them a harmful way to handle stress.

When a youngster sees someone stabbed on TV, it has little meaning until he seeks to relieve the pain of his inability to handle a stressful relationship. If he has not the strength to bear the pain until he figures out what to do, he may imitate TV and relieve his own pain by hurting another.

As a result of TV, children are more aware of what is going on, but the problem is that *they have not the internal strength to handle this awareness*. They are socially more aware but less capable of socially mature behavior. Making children aware of drugs and sex does not mean that they can handle those things. It only means they are aware of them. Intellectual knowledge and understanding are not the same as the strength to handle a problem. An alcoholic knows he is hurting his life; he understands what he is doing; he lacks the internal strength to stop drinking.

TV is entertaining. That is good. TV shows the experts, the pros, the very best. That is good. But TV does not show the work involved in becoming an expert. That is bad. TV does not show the drudgery and hours of practice it takes to succeed. TV creates a temporary sense of happiness, and that may be good, but TV also implies that it is wrong to ever be unhappy, and that is bad.

It is here that some real misfortune and heartache lies. When problems arise in real life, we cannot just change channels. *Excessive TV-watching is the villian, not* selective TV-watching.

In addition to creating a world of illusions, TV isolates the excessive viewer. With his week of watching carefully planned, the fanatic no longer knows or cares what those around him are doing. Children are told to "keep the noise down" because mom and dad are watching TV. Many families watch TV for hours, saying nothing to each other. Ultimately, the heavy viewer becomes conditioned to passivity. Involvement with others becomes hard work and risky. Sooner or later his interpersonal relationships begin to deteriorate. A wife gets fed up with it all, turns to her husband and says "You never take me out any more." "You never talk to me like you used to." Weekends are lost in watching endless football games.

To use TV or to abuse TV; that is the question. Relaxing and watching a ball game is one thing; but when the game becomes more important than those around you, loneliness is the inevitable result.

The real concern should be what the act of watching TV—the very process of passively sitting and viewing—is doing to us as social human beings.

I believe that no matter how good the program, no matter how relaxing, entertaining or educational, television is the main (but not the only) cause of loneliness in our country today. I believe excessive TV viewing is having a disastrous effect on us as human beings. Never before in history have people been so immobilized for such long periods of time.

The effects of TV can be summarized as follows:

1. *TV is a passive process*. The pleasure received comes from passive behavior. There is no physical and little mental activity involved. The enjoyment does not

last. All human pleasures that last and build internal strength require some effort on the part of the person. Even yoga and meditation require mental and physical effort. Thus TV viewers are less inclined to seek pleasure through active pursuits when, without any effort, passive pleasure is found by turning on a switch.

2. *TV is noncreative for the viewer.* It does not teach him to be imaginative or to think. All the creativity is in the tube. The producer, director, writer, actor—they are the creative ones. If the viewer, after the show, discusses the ideas presented, then the show acts as a stimulant. But only rarely does TV require creative thinking by the viewer.

3. *TV immobilizes or physically limits the viewer.* The automobile has drastically cut the amount of walking we do. Now TV is reducing our physical activity even more. Sitting for hours in front of a TV set is turning us into a nation of sitters. Add to this the amount of nonnutritional food that we eat during an evening's viewing, and the disastrous effect on our health is obvious.

4. *TV gives the viewer no lasting sense of value or accomplishment.* To gain value from what we do, it must be something that requires active effort. TV requires no effort. Thus the time spent watching TV gives nothing to those who are lonely and need a sense of worth, value, and confidence in themselves. Preschool children need to spend time developing worth, and yet they spend more time than anyone in front of the tube.

5. *TV does not build the strength we need to handle life's stresses.* Whole families watch TV and have the idea that it is a beneficial family activity. After all, they are all together. So are dead bodies in a cemetery. There is none of the human interaction that is required if family strength is to be built. TV does nothing to build strength (unless it

is used as an hour's relaxation from the tensions of the day).

6. *Most important, TV creates loneliness.* Excessive watching tends to cut us off from others. It is a nonsocializing process. TV is a time-filler. For many, it provides an escape, but an escape to boredom.

In order to learn how to get along with others, *we must learn the skills of speaking and listening.* These skills must be worked at every day. Just as a piano player or tennis player must practice his skills, so these socializing skills must be continually developed.

TV is especially deceiving when it becomes involved in personal relationships. Although two people may spend a lot of time together in front of the set, there is no meaningful involvement between them. They are lulled into a false sense of security about their relationships. When the TV goes off, getting along is more difficult because they have not had much involvement with each other. No strength to handle stress has been built into the relationship.

Lonely people have said that, without TV, they would be bored to tears. TV is their primary source of entertainment, information, news, romance and—what is worse—their chief source of emotional involvement. It is their window to the world.

Instead of developing their own sense of identity and self-worth, they identify with superstars, celebrities, and TV personalities. Their expectations are raised accordingly. Whatever they achieve in the real world is found to be lacking in comparison to the accomplishments of TV's super-heroes. The result? A reinforced sense of inadequacy and failure and loneliness.

A rather unattractive, forty-two-year-old woman called for an appointment one day. She said it was urgent. Beth was lonely and needed to talk to someone. When she was offered an appointment in the early afternoon, she said she could not take it because she would miss her favorite soap opera. She could come in later, which she did.

Beth said she lived alone. She was out of work but was getting unemployment benefits which she used to pay the rent, buy groceries, and so on. Since she was not working, there was no reason to get up early. She slept until noon. Then she would get up, fix lunch, and watch TV. She said the soap operas were good and she could relate to the problems the people had. After that, the late afternoon movie came on. After the movie, Beth would call her mother and then her sister. That took an hour, and then she would eat dinner, watch the news, make the bed, and do the dishes. By then it would be approaching seven or seven-thirty. That is prime time, so it was back to the couch and TV. After all the late talk-shows were over, she would go to bed. That had been her schedule ever since she gave up looking for a job. No risk, no stress, and no wonder that she felt lonely and depressed.

Beth began to make changes by joining a neighborhood bowling league with her sister. Later I got her into some volunteer work at a youth rehabilitation center. She enjoyed this so much, she ultimately decided to return to college for a degree in social work.

Consider the amount of time you spend watching TV. Make a study of the amount of time your TV set is on each day and each week. Think about the things you enjoy doing with others. Think about your friends and how often you see them. Walk away from that TV. Get involved.

Happiness comes from involvement. The real fun is always in doing things yourself—not in watching others or watching TV.

Chapter twelve

Suicide, the ultimate act of loneliness

Is suicide a hostile act? A last chance to get even with the world? Or is it a cowardly act; or perhaps an act of courage? Is it rational or irrational? An act of anger, defiance, or antagonism? Or is it the supreme gesture of helplessness?

All these theories and questions about suicide have been presented at one time or another. But in essence, when a person takes his own life, he is saying that he sees no way to lead a sufficiently satisfying life. The ultimate act of a lonely person is to take his own life. He gives up because to do so is less painful than continuing to experience failure. He sees nothing in the future except more misery and more agony.

The reason a person does anything is because, at the time he does it, he believes it to be the best choice open to him. Choices are weighed by the amount of pain or pleasure connected with them. If a person feels bad, he will look for something to reduce the pain. If he feels good, he will continue what he has been doing.

A suicidal person seeks a way out, a way to escape pain. He sees only two alternatives: to continue his present suffering or to take his own life. If he chooses suicide, he takes what he believes to be his best choice. He thinks that continuing to live would be more painful.

In such a time of crisis and stress, a person's internal strength is severely tested. People who have developed self-confidence and inner strength do not commit suicide, because their strength gives them the ability to cope with the problems of life. Even in the face of extreme adversity or death, people with a strong identity exhibit a sense of grace and self-dignity.

If a lonely person is convinced no one really cares about him, he begins to limit himself. He feels depressed. He believes he has little or no control over what is happening to him. He begins to choose less successful pathways of fulfilling his basic needs. The pain of loneliness, failure, and rejection overwhelm him, and in desperation he turns inward to the last person he can have as a friend—himself. Then he makes more and more poor choices, all of which lead him away from the happiness he seeks.

He may choose to become involved with an emotion like depression. Depression, as well as other choices, then serves as an excuse for his inability to change and to live his life more effectively. Other choices include self-involvement with physical symptoms, such as backaches, migraine headaches, or ulcers. Aggressive, acting-out, seemingly uncontrollable behavior are other forms of self-involvement.

Finally, if the pain of loneliness and failure becomes too great, the person may choose to go into his own head, to become crazy or psychotic. If he is not willing to live with these choices, then he may decide to become involved with an addiction like drugs or alcohol, which serve to relieve the pain he feels. Sooner or later, regardless of whether he makes all, some, or none of the above choices, he may decide on suicide as the only way.

But no matter what the decision, the individual is still responsibile for what he does. He is not really sick. A person does not choose to be sick. A syphillitic spirochete eating at the brain, a brain tumor or a blow to the head—all these *are not choices. They happen.* But the painful feeling of loneliness tells him he lacks the warmth of human relationships and the worth and dignity as a person. What he chooses to do to rid himself of this painful feeling is the best choice he believes is available to him. The choice of living, of being a person who has value, of having meaningful lasting relationships—this he believes is not possible for him. Ultimately, he makes what he thinks is the only choice left to him—suicide.

The person who is seriously thinking of suicide is caught in the dilemma shown in Figure 21.

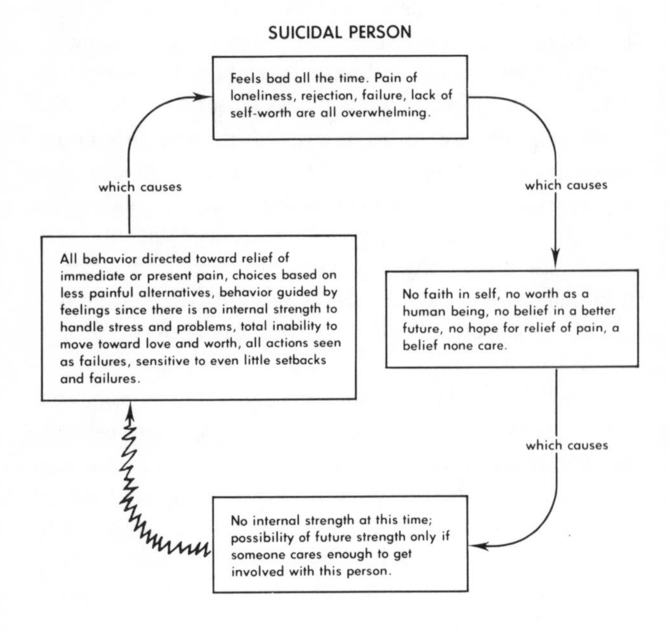

Figure 21

Sadness engulfs him. He looks at himself objectively and rationally evaluates his life. He sees no hope in any short- or long-range plans. Furthermore, the longer he feels bad, the more his internal strength ebbs away. It becomes easier to give up the struggle than to keep on trying.

If you are trying to help someone who is thinking about suicide, you are trying to get them to see they have a chance to lead a better life. The problem is that you have faith in the future, but the person you are talking to does not. He feels bad; you do not. The person whose life has tremenduous sadness is under great stress.

Suicidal persons often exhibit some of the following traits.

1. They cannot handle time; they live in the immediate present and cannot plan for tomorrow.
2. They do not see much humor in life.
3. They are often unreasonable and difficult to talk to. They withdraw.
4. They cannot tolerate the pain of failure; each little failure is a major crisis.
5. They are not flexible.
6. They do not have much internal strength and confidence in their own ability to succeed in life.
7. They do not see many options. They feel trapped. They alienate themselves from others.

The suicidal person has tried to succeed in life, but has experienced rejection and failure. He may have tried the emotional companions of anger and depression. Or he may have tried physical companions such as backaches, colitis, or ulcers. Perhaps he may even have tried addictions like alcohol, food, gambling, or drugs. After trying one or more of these alternatives and still finding nothing to relieve his pain, he begins to see suicide as the only remaining option.

Thus, he commits suicide because he has concluded that his life is hopeless. Some observers, seeing this hoplessness in suicide victims, have concluded that suicide is an act of cowardice. But killing one's self is never easy; it is just seen as a less painful alternative. The suicidal person's basic goal is to end his pain. What causes the pain is his inability to find love and worth. He doesn't know what to do. Whatever he tries does not help. Because he is not able to succeed, the pain of loneliness and failure increases.

For instance, a very wealthy, prominent man who suddenly loses his reputation and money may feel so bad that he thinks it would be better for him if he were to commit suicide than to continue to live in misery. What is more, he doubts his future will ever be any better. He says his life will never be the same again. If he had hope, he would cling to life, believing things would get better. This is where a person's internal strength comes in, and where a supportive, loving family and good friends really count. If you need strength, your family and friends can provide that strength until you regain your perspective on life. They help you through the crisis.

Other people may find a serious physical illness suddenly thrust upon them, like a crippling disease or blindness. If they think the future holds nothing for them, they may commit suicide.

The way people look at suicide has changed dramatically since the turn of the century. At one time, it was viewed primarily in religious terms, as a sin. It was said that only God should take a life. A more recent view is that suicide is a form of mental illness. The term "illness" placed suicide in a medical framework and implied an uncontrollable physiological cause. That relieved a person of responsibility for his own behavior because it was not his fault if he had an illness that was mental. Illness also meant that drugs could be used to cure the condition. So suicidal patients were heavily sedated. What they needed was the belief that someone cared about them. They were given a pill. They had no one who really cared about them. They felt worthless and helpless.

Sometimes suicide-prone people are sent to a mental hospital for a rest. These people have simply taken on more in life than they can handle. Sometimes it is beneficial for such people to take a rest; when they come back, they are more able to handle the problems of daily living.

The secret in coming back successfully is to do those things that build internal strength and to take stress in small steps. You do not learn to handle life again by jumping right back into the explosive situation that caused the upset in the first place. You learn to handle stress gradually.

The idea of suicide as a rational act is becoming widely accepted. The view that it is an individual decision is no longer disregarded. Some even speculate that it is the person's right. Others maintain no one has the right to take his own life.

There are many more suicide attempts than there are actual suicides. One estimate is that only one attempt in ten results in death. Some persons who try to kill themselves are admitted to hospitals for other reasons, and some are cared for by their families because of the social stigma involved.

There are also a growing number of people who have never made an attempt at suicide but have comtemplated or threatened it. Both the number of threats and the number of attempts are increasing at a rapid rate. Suicide is the second leading cause of death among teenagers, second only to accidental death.

The other day my daughter came home and said that one of her girl friends was having a tough time at school. She asked what she could do to help her friend Elaine. She said the kids in school had been ridiculing Elaine about her clothes, and Elaine had gotten angry and told off a couple of them. Now this group of kids would not talk to her. The silent treatment. This had been going on for several days. Elaine cried and carried on and told her mother she was going to kill herself.

Elaine was having a hard time, but it was only temporary. I told my daughter the best way she could help right now was to be Elaine's friend. In doing that, Elaine would see that she still had a friend and would feel a little better. Young people forget quickly; by next week, everything would probably be back to normal.

Sooner or later all of those involved would make up. But Elaine would learn the art of friendship if someone would show her how through caring about her. As my daughter worked at making friends with Elaine, both girls would continue to develop the skills needed in making friends. To Elaine the crisis of the moment undoubtedly appeared insurmountable; yet it would pass with time. But to a depressed person overwhelmed with the pain of loneliness and failure, this is not apparent.

To some people, even the topic of suicide is very disturbing. They get uncomfortable talking or reading about it. Others are fascinated by it. Many do not understand suicide or the pain found in extreme loneliness and failure. They ask why someone would want to kill himself. They point to people young and old who have fought against overwhelming odds to save their lives. However, those people have the desire to live. They believe that life is worthwhile. What is difficult to understand and extremely hard to deal with is the person who gives up hope and no longer wants to live. Those whose lives are filled with love and worth have never experienced the hopeless, devastating feelings of long-term loneliness.

Although there are many causes or reasons why people commit suicide, there is a definite common element in all suicides: to the person involved it is the least painful choice in a tremendously complicated, unhappy life. If a person is really determined to commit suicide, he will be very hard to stop. Sooner or later, if that is what he wants, he will succeed in taking his life.

Often people who attempt suicide are medicated until they "feel better." Medication does not teach responsible living. It is not a cure, only a temporary relief. However, to a few it allows a temporary period to recoup; and if the family members become aware of the person's crisis situation, they can become more involved and supportive. Many times in first attempts at suicide, this is the goal the unhappy person has in mind. They need help, and this is their way of trying to get it. They are, in essence, saying to the world, "Look at me. My life is all wrong. I'm lonely. I need help. Somebody notice me. Somebody help me."

It is warm personal involvement that helps the lonely person see his life in more worthwhile terms. Medication is helpful only if it allows those who care to gain access to the person. Only then does the person give up the idea of taking his own life, because he is helped to see better alternatives.

Many people who are hospitalized for attempting suicide commit suicide later. The first attempts are cries for help; if no one answers those cries, the suicidal person becomes more desperate. An attempted suicide is a warning signal a lonely person sends out, asking someone to help him. Suicidal people often do not realize that others are trying to reach them; somehow, all too often, the message or connection is not made, and this is unfortunate.

Loneliness is one of the major concerns of suicidal persons. A tremendous sense of failure is another. A future with no hope is unbearable. They will often telephone friends or even strangers before they try to kill themselves. They will leave notes for loved ones, call radio stations, talk to telephone operators, or even dial a number at random. They are clinging to life by a thread and are hoping to find someone who cares. They may know many people and still be lonely because in their minds they do not feel those people are real friends who truly care about them. Sometimes the suicidal person does not know anyone well and is all alone in a world where everyone seems to have someone.

As suicide-prone people become deeply involved with the four major self-destroying addictions—hard narcotics, alcohol, food, and gambling—they will need help. It is better if people with these addictions become involved in a program where there are people available to talk to them at all hours. Programs such as Alcoholics Anonymous or Weight Watchers are very helpful. Private counseling in itself is helpful, but it should be used in addition to a total program designed for the particular addiction.

Age is often an important consideration in suicide. There are more suicides in the over-sixty age group than in any other group, although there are indications of an increase in suicides among teenagers. As people get older, they find their habits set and changes in the world more disturbing. They have less and less hope of achieving all the dreams and aspirations they had in their youth. Also, in old age, one partner often dies while the other lives on. Loneliness in old age can be severe. Rest homes can be pleasant, but they can also be dehumanizing and terribly lonely. To be alone after years of being close to a loved one in marriage can make a person feel extremely depressed, especially if few relatives visit.

When you are young, it is easy to accept life as it comes. It is also much easier to get involved with others. As you grow older, you tend to look at your own life in terms of increased worries and anxieties about a multitude of things you never thought of earlier. Economic problems and feelings of loneliness, anxiety, boredom and illness become more pronounced.

Another important consideration in suicide is marital status. Suicide rates are much higher among single people. The reason is simple: as a rule married people have a higher degree of personal involvement in their lives. Most marriages offer opportunities for involvement, which reduces loneliness and alienation. Many clients have told me they are unhappily married but would never think of divorce because they would be too lonely and would lose what little love they have.

It is also interesting to note that an individual can change. In a different time, different place, and different situation, *where stress is not as great,* the person may no longer think of suicide. For him, the crisis is over. It is like some jobs; certain ones you like and you function quite well in, but there are others which you just could not tolerate. When you do not function well, you are under tremendous stress. A change of environment and situation along with the individual's increased efforts to change his life can do wonders in helping him find happiness.

Suicide prevention centers are becoming more common through-out the country. They are crisis-oriented, and a person needing assistance can call for help. A hot line or help line gives a person a place to call when he has nowhere else to turn.

Sometimes a person in the early stages of a crisis is attracted to this type of agency because he can talk to someone who cares without relatives finding out and causing a scene.

In such a situation, the person who answers does not have any involvement with the person who calls. They are both just voices on the phone. They have never met. The telephone counselor tries to build a little involvement by searching for something in the caller's life that is positive. Sometimes this is hard because the person feels so bad that all he wants to talk about is how bad he feels.

The same is true when a friend or relative calls you and says he is thinking about committing suicide. He is calling because of all the bad things that are happening to him. If you dwell on the bad things, you make him feel worse. You will reinforce his feelings of failure. But if you go too far in pushing the good life, the person will think you are unsympathetic and cut you off. You have to search for the happy medium where you keep him on the phone and build positive involvement. You have got to search for something good in his life. You talk to him in hopes that he will begin to see some hope of a better future. You help him start to build a place in the world, something that will be better to do than killing himself.

Talking in person is much better than talking over the phone. Try to get the person to come in and see you or let you arrange for him to see a counselor. You have to be careful not to break the involvement you have started but at the same time to get the person to come in for more help.

Burdens that appear to be overwhelming never seem so large when they are shared with someone who cares. That is important—caring. People contemplating suicide who call a crisis center will say things like, "What do you care? You don't even know me." They doubt that anyone cares at all. They may say, "My life doesn't matter. No one knows I'm alive. I could die today and no one would miss me." These people are extremely lonely and uninvolved. They need people.

In talking to people about suicide, it is important not to get into a discussion about why they want to commit suicide. That only serves to dredge up all their past failures and limits the conversation to suicide. It gives suicide credence.

A good approach is to say something along these lines: "I think I can help you, but I can't help if you kill yourself. Let's see if we can work things out. I think we can. At least, let's give it a try." And then go on to talk about something else. Don't dwell on suicide; and don't say, "Well, if you're planning to kill yourself, why are you talking to me?" That would be a bit rough for anyone to take. It is better to come across in a supportive, low-profile fashion: "I think there are some things I can do to help. Why don't you give us a chance to try and work it out?" You might even say, "You can always kill yourself. Let's try for a while longer and see what we can work out together."

You have to be careful not to give the impression that you do not care. You have to convey warmth and involvement. You are in essence offering him your strength for a while. You say things like "together" and "try" and "We'll see if we can work it out." In doing so, he no longer feels he is alone. You are offering to get involved, which is what he really needs.

If the person persists in wanting to talk about suicide, you might say, "I don't know anything about suicide." You do not want to get into a long discussion of suicide; that only encourages a person to try it. Suicidal people are literally crying out for involvement of any kind. What you want to do is to offer them this positive involvement. By talking about suicide, depression, and loneliness, you are validating their failures. You are confirming what they fear.

Quite often, people will try to tell a depressed, suicidal person about all the bright tomorrows and what a rosy world it is. It is better never to offer unlimited hope or false promises to people who are down and out. They will not believe you. What you must do is to get them to make a small plan, centered around something they like. You must help them to take each day as it comes and not rehash the past. As they see a glimmer of hope on the immediate horizon and as they gain strength from you, they will begin to realize some joy in living.

If you cannot get them to make a plan, just talk about as many pleasant things as you can, such as what they are interested in. That is a good form of positive involvement, and sometimes in a crisis that is all the person needs to get him through to another tomorrow. There is no magic in preventing suicide, unless it is in the caring. If we care, there is hope. If we do not care, who else will?

Chapter thirteen

Seeking professional help

Sometimes it is difficult to find the right kind of help when you need it. If your car is not working properly, finding a good mechanic can be a problem. Who can you trust? Does he know what he is doing? Does he overcharge? Looking in the Yellow Pages can get you a list of names, but how can you tell who really knows what he is doing?

If you think finding a good mechanic is hard, you should try finding someone who is qualified to help you live your life more effectively and more happily. What about private counselors? How about public agencies or friends? How do you know who can really help you? If you are extremely lonely, the variety of people to whom you can turn is probably endless. Social worker? Psychiatrist? Psychologist? Rehabilitation counselor? Doctor? Lawyer? Bartender? Girl friend? Boy friend? Neighbor? Mental health clinic? Public or private agency? Who knows where to go?

Obviously, the reason anyone seeks professional help is that he cannot solve his problem by himself. What he basically wants to know is, "Who can help me feel better about myself and my life?" There are also other questions to be considered: Is the person qualified? Is he more qualified because there is a college degree after his name? Does state certification really mean he can help me or has he just passed a state test?

Not all the doubts and questions end there, for once you start in counseling, you continually ask yourself questions: Is my life changing? Is this counselor really helping me? I wonder if he keeps me coming just to take my money? Does he really care about me or am I just another case in his overcrowded counseling schedule? What does he really think about me? About my problems?

There are some basic guidelines which can be a great help to those who are lonely and depressed as they look for a good counselor. Too many people approach a counselor with awe, as if he were a powerful, all-knowing figure. Get away from this super human concept of a counselor. He is still a human being. So if he is going to help you, he should come across as believable and honest.

Ask your counselor questions. Constructive therapy and counseling is a two-way street. Hiding behind the mask of anonymity is an outdated approach to counseling. It certainly does not help two people communicate. How can a counselor help you if he doesn't care enough to share some of his own experiences with you? It is not that you want to hear all about his life; it is that you want some human involvement. Two people ought to be working together to try to solve real problems. Isn't this why you seek a counselor, or at least what you expect from him—warmth, kindness, understanding, and help?

Furthermore, not every counselor can help every client. Many clients have been to other counselors before coming to me. On the other hand, I am sure there are some clients who I have tried to help who later received more help from other counselors. This does not mean I feel inadequate. I did try. I just could not get through to that particular person at that time.

Counseling is a demanding profession that takes skill and creative thinking ability. People come because they have tough problems. If they were easy to solve, the people would not seek counseling.

No one comes in to say, "My life is going along so well right now. Let's figure out why." I am asked to help overcome obstacles they, their families, and their friends have not been able to handle yet.

Loneliness can be overcome primarily by creative help. Creativity and caring are important traits of good counselors. These attributes are developed through years of counseling. After adequate education a counselor really learns to counsel by counseling. The more he counsels, the more likely he is to help others. You would not ask a beginner to tune a car for the Indy 500. You look for experience.

One of the best yardsticks you can use to determine whether a counselor is qualified to help you is to talk to those who have already been to see him. Ask them if they received help. Ask them if their life is any better. If you were buying a used car, you would want to talk to the previous owner. We check out stores by talking with people who shop there. Fine restaurants gain their good reputations by people who tell others about the good food they have had there. Many products such as washers and dryers, TVs or cars, are purchased mainly on the reputation of the company's service department. At one time I bought electrical appliances for our house wherever I could get the best price. After several bad experiences in trying to get service, I now buy from one dealer because he gives us excellent service.

Counselors who help people live their life more effectively actually gain a reputation in much the same way. If a mental health bureau, counseling agency, or an individual counselor in private practice is doing a good job, the word gets around soon enough. By the same token, an agency or individual doing a poor job of counseling soon develops a poor reputation.

Before you decide on a counselor, you might try to find out how he is living his own life. A counselor who has a great many personal problems in maintaining his own family relationships would hardly make a good marriage counselor. He knows little about how to sustain an intimate marital relationship over any period of time. It is better to get help from someone who has himself found happiness in married life.

A person who has never been married would have limited background and understanding to draw upon in helping a married person improve his marriage. A person whose children are constantly in serious trouble might not be the ideal counselor for parents and teenagers.

Those who join Alcoholics Anonymous tend to succeed in putting their life back together because their counselors are former alcoholics. They have learned by experience how to stop drinking. Their job in counseling alcoholics is to draw on their own real-life experiences in order to help others do the same. You feel more confident because you know they've been through what you're going through, and they have made it.

But how can you tell if a counselor is helping you once you have been going to him for a while? One criterion is if you believe he really and truly cares about you as a human being. When you no longer feel that you are just his two o'clock appointment, then that counselor is helping you.

Does he show he has faith in you? Does he really believe your life will be better? A person who has little faith in your ability to change your life cannot do much for you. If he agrees that you are hopeless or do not have much ability, then he is not going to help you feel better about yourself. This kind of counselor makes you feel inferior. The last thing you need is another person who doubts your ability to do anything with your life.

If your counselor does not have faith in you, then who will? If you had enough faith in your ability to work things out alone, you probably would not need a counselor in the first place. Do you find your counselor easy to talk to? Do you have the natural ease and enjoyment which comes from talking naturally with another person who is interested in what you are doing? A good counselor keeps the conversation flowing and finds things to talk about. After several visits you should begin to really enjoy talking to your counselor.

A good counselor helps you achieve some goal you have in mind. He helps you change what you want to change. Somehow during this process you begin to see your counselor less and less as a counselor and more and more as a friend.

Friendship here should not be an emotional ''I-love-you'' type of attachment but an honest, sincere relationship. You do not have to go bowling together to be friends. But you are not going to overcome loneliness by going to a counselor who is cold and indifferent and just sees his clients as appointments on his calendar.

You want a counselor who is going to be honest with you, but you want a form of honesty that does not downgrade and humiliate you. Warmth, courtesy, and concern are the kinds of things that should develop between two people trying to solve a problem together. Empathy is also important, but it should never be used as a crutch, like sympathy, to condone irresponsible behavior.

Besides being honest, counselors have to be optimists. They have to have faith in their clients and never give up trying. A good counselor helps by getting you moving toward other people so you are not totally dependent on him. Theoretical solutions to problems are seldom applicable to everyday life, where issues are complex. You want practical, relevant solutions.

You might ask yourself what specific behaviors your counselor exhibits toward you. This will give you some understanding into his attitude toward you. Does he smile at you when you see each other? Is he friendly toward you? Does he make you feel welcome? Does he give you the feeling he has faith in you? Does he take the time to see you? Is he late or on time? Is he critical of you?

A good counseling session always has some laughter in it. Laughter is magic in making you feel better. Some people feel bad because they have not laughed in years. They come to counseling and could fill the entire time with their sadness and misery. If there is no laughter but a lot of crying, then it is doubtful how valuable that counselor will be in helping you find a better life.

What about the counselor's office? Is it a friendly sort of place? Or is it one of those antiseptic, sterile-looking places? Does the receptionist make you feel you are important when you come in? Do they seem glad to see you, or do they look at you with that look that says, "Not you again." Is the office furniture arranged in a manner that is conducive to friendly conversation or do you sit opposite each other across a big desk?

People talk more freely when they sit in a cordial manner, as they would if they were visiting each other's homes. After all, when you go to a counselor, it is not like going to a bank for a loan. There is a time to be personal and a time to be impersonal. Counseling is a personal business. You are confiding things to your counselor that you would not tell anyone.

One young couple referred by their gynecologist said they had been arguing all the time. They were in their early twenties. Both worked. She was an editor on a suburban newspaper and he was a pharmacist. The young lady, Jeanie, started out by saying, "We know we shouldn't argue, but it's all we seem to do." Chuck said that on the way home from work every night he would say to himself over and over again, "Don't argue. Don't argue." And yet when he got home, somehow, sooner or later, they wound up arguing. This couple had been to a counselor who told them not to fight. He gave them good advice. He said, "Don't argue, and your marriage will get better."

This is an example of well-intentioned advice, but this kind of advice will not help anyone build a happier life or change what he is doing. It is negative counseling. It is the easiest to do, but the least effective. A good counselor should help you figure out what to do that is better than what you are doing. That is positive counseling. And that is the key.

It is hard to do things differently even when you know you should. That is why Chuck and Jeanie came in. They could not figure out what to do on their own. They wanted to stop fighting and had tried everything they could think of. Now it was up to all of us to figure out a better alternative.

We did not waste any time sitting around discussing what they had been arguing about or whose fault it was that they were so miserable. We began discussing some of the positive things they like to do together. They knew how to fight. They did not need any lessons in that, and simply telling them to stop would not do any good. Everyone had already told them that.

Chuck and Jeanie remembered things they had not done for several years, such as riding bicycles together. This is where a good counselor comes in. He helps people look at what they are doing and evaluate it in terms of what they want out of life. Then they plan better ways of achieving those objectives. After this couple began to do some pleasant things together, the arguments began to lessen. In several weeks, they were on the road to a much better life.

If you have been going to a counselor three or four months and there is no sign of change in your life, perhaps that particular counselor is not going to help you at that time in your life. Several months is long enough for anyone to have some impact on another. Actually, you should begin to see *some change* after the first three or four weeks. Your life may not automatically become happy and totally effecitve after a number of sessions, but something should be getting better. You should be feeling better about yourself. If nothing is changed, you should be looking elsewhere for help.

I have had some clients for years, but there has generally been some change in what they do and how they feel within the first month or two. The fact that someone goes to counseling for years is not bad. Remember that a counselor is a teacher as well as a friend. He teaches us how to live our life more effectively. Many professionals employ coaches all their professional life. Why would it be so strange for someone to want to work continually at living their life more effectively, especially if the help they have received has been effective?

A fairly attractive, middle-aged woman by the name of Terry, whose husband died of cancer, came in for counseling. She was lonely and had no one to turn to, as they had no children. She was barely making a living evenings as a waitress. Terry had poured out her troubles to anyone who would listen. She had tried her boss, co-workers, and occasionally even a sympathetic customer would lend an ear; but no one had helped her begin to change her life.

That is the problem with merely listening; although it is part of counseling, listening by itself cannot help a person to plan better things he or she could do. If you go to a counselor who just listens to you, can he really help?

Terry told how nice everyone was and how sympathetically they listened. But she said that somehow, in spite of all these friends, she felt she was getting worse. She said she did not even go to the beauty parlor anymore. She did not call anyone because, she said, "They don't really care about me."

We thought of some things she might like to do. These included her joining a bowling league and a singles club, and serving two mornings a week as a volunteer in the city hospital. Terry started with the volunteer work and later joined the club. Several months after that in the fall, she joined a bowling league. As Terry began to change what she was doing, her life began to change. After a while, she was too busy to be lonely.

A good counselor does not tell you what to do. He does not promise you heaven on earth or pretend to have all the answers. He does not force his own value judgments on you. Value judgments about what you do in your life should be up to you. It is the counselor's job to help you look more objectively at what you are doing and for areas of strength to build on. Also, he should help you plan how to go about making changes in your life.

If a counselor overindulges you by listening to you cry repeatedly about how bad your life is, several things will result: (1) it will definitely reinforce the belief you already have that your life is in bad shape; (2) it will make you feel worse; and (3) it will definitely postpone any meaningful change in your life because you will spend all your time talking about the depressing side of your life.

If you really want to begin to live differently from the way you have been living, then you have got to get on with it. No more excuses or postponements. No alibis. If something does not work out, try something else. Try another plan. Try another day. Try another time, another place. Just don't give up. If you get depressed, so you are depressed. You can be depressed and still change what you are doing. Ultimately as you change what you are doing, your depression will leave.

There are several basic choices in everyone's life: live with what is bothering you, get rid of it, or change it. If you are going to change it, then think of a plan and put it to work. It is in the doing that you will begin to grow and feel good as a person.

An executive in a large department store came into my office one afternoon. He had spent $1,100 with a large counseling firm in New York where he had gone seeking professional help. Mike said that when he first went to New York, he was given an extensive series of psychological tests. There were written tests, oral exams, projective techniques where he filled in the blanks—the works. When the tests were all over, he received very little counseling. They told him the test results showed that he was suffering from inadequate personality development. They said he was a "passive-dependent personality." When he asked what that meant, they replied he was excessively dependent upon others because of the way his mother brought him up.

Some counselors think that is all they have to do: diagnose the clients' problems and place a label on them. I do not think that is the answer. It did not help Mike much to know he was a passive-dependent personality. It actually further reduced his already low opinion of himself and provided him with a solid excuse for not accepting the responsibility for changing his life. If his $1,100 had been spent on a good vacation cruise, he would have been way ahead.

Don't be afraid to ask what the charge is for the counseling services. A good counselor demonstrates financially ethical behavior. He does not overcharge because he thinks that is what the traffic will bear. He should have established rates and be able to quote them to prospective clients who call exploring whether or not they want to come to him for help and guidance.

Don't ever be afraid of terminating your sessions with your counselor. He should be a person who is there *when you need him*. Your goal and his should be that of the earliest practical solution to your problems and of rendering you able subsequently to solve problems yourself.

Remember, there is no magic in seeing someone once a week for an hour. Some counseling sessions last forty-five minutes, some only twenty minutes. Some of my clients come in twice a month, some every two months, and others just call periodically. And don't be afraid to go back. You should think of a counselor as a friend. Some clients will come back every six months, and we discuss what they are doing in their lives and where they see themselves. We laugh a lot together as we look back at how bad things used to be. These sessions are valuable and really help in gaining perspective and sustaining growth.

Finally, although a counselor is a friend, all friendships have their limitations. I have friends I only see on the tennis court. Others I see socially at parties. Many I would not want to live with. So, too, with your counselor. Calling him at three in the morning or expecting him to mix with you socially may be asking too much. All friendships are limited and part of growing relationally is to learn how to respect these limitations.

Sometimes group counseling offers advantages which cannot be found in a one-to-one counseling situation. Groups that have some common interests are good. Also groups are good if you get the feeling that others care for you and that you are not alone. The actual application of group therapy is the same as individual counseling—to make a plan and work it out. The plans are individual ones. Sometimes the group helps you plan, but the basic procedure in many groups is to help you plan to do something outside the group.

What is important in a group is that its members get together, learn to accept each other, talk reasonably about their problems, and come up with tentative, realistic solutions. It is not the actual solving of specific problems but the human interaction that is important. It is in this warm climate of involvement that a person grows, builds internal strength, and begins to think about what he can do to solve his own problems.

The secret of group therapy is in the process, which is also true of individual therapy. The only difference in a group is that you are with more people, and it is often more fun and interesting because there are many more variables. In a good group, things begin to happen among the people. There is a certain climate that develops in a group; if the persons in it handle the meeting realistically and well, they all gain in strength. If a person is lonely, group therapy will often help.

Interest groups are excellent ways to meet other people and get involved beyond your immediate circle of friends. Growth groups or counseling groups, if run properly, are not merely a means of seeking others who have the same problems. They are not the "misery loves company" type of thing. A good group, regardless of what type it is, is based on a caring atmosphere. This is reflected in the group leader's attentiveness and in how he responds to what is said, as well as in the actions of the individual members of the group.

It is not usually therapeutic to bare one's soul in a group. The basis of all group therapy is the development of social skills that a person can use to move out into the world on his own and do some worthwhile things. A group that forces participants to bare embarrassing parts of their lives is not productive. Confession may be good for the soul, as some say, but in this circumstance it is not good for one's self-image. You should never be asked to do anything phony, artificial, or embarrassing. When you see your close friends or meet other people, you do not act phony. Groups should be like real life if they are to be of value.

As I mentioned earlier, one of the most successful groups today is Alcoholics Anonymous. A.A. typifies involvement and caring. Members can call a fellow A.A. member at two o'clock in the morning if they need help.

The friend goes to him, stays with him, maybe plays cards with him, and helps see him through his crisis. This builds a tremenduous allegiance among individual members. They care. They know they can call for help because the person at the other end cares. A.A. offers friendship and caring, which gives the members strength. One or two people supply their internal strength until the other person gains enough strength to make it on his own. What do they talk about in the A.A. groups? Mostly about what a person can do instead of drinking. They talk about what they have done to avoid drinking—not about how to get drunk.

In essence, a lonely person looking for help should see if he finds these things in the group he joins: he feels that he is not alone and that others care for him; that he finds that he is developing the strength to handle more stress, that he is more self-disciplined; he finds himself making plans in terms of what he can do to live his life more effectively; he finds others with whom he can talk about common interests; he finds persons who listen; he finds himself beginning to take an interest in others, in what they do and in his ability to communicate with them; his own life outside the group begins to take on a greater meaning. If these things become apparent to him over a period of time, he is in a good group.

Chapter fourteen

Living creatively

An unhappy person living with the pain of loneliness finds it difficult to think creatively because he is overwhelmed with all his painful feelings. The sheer weight of problems, either real or imagined, is enormous. He is overly sensitive to criticism given and advice offered. Instead of thinking about solutions to problems, he looks for excuses or reasons for not succeeding.

A former student of mine came in recently and said she was miserable. Her boss was giving her a hard time at work; her younger sister had a lot of problems and she was trying to help her; she was arguing with her boy friend; and her parents were fighting. She said courses at the university were more difficult than usual, and she was worried about her grades. Mary Ellen was facing so many problems she did not know where to begin. When she looked at her life, the weight of the problems immobilized her creative thought processes.

Mary Ellen and I started on the easiest problem she had. She was carrying far too many subjects at the university and was working full-time. She said she had to work, so we figured out a way she could reduce the number of courses she was taking. That would enable her to focus her energy and get better grades. Finding a place to begin, where success can be experienced, is the key. Mary Ellen saw all her problems at once, and her mind could not handle that.

In subsequent sessions we talked about her younger sister and what she could do to help her. I suggested she spend time with her, perhaps doing something enjoyable. Mary Ellen suggested taking her to the shopping mall and going for bike rides. As her school work and her relationship with her sister began to improve, she began to handle other problems on her own.

The ability to focus on our needs one at a time is important. Actually, facing reality creatively is the key. But is is like the old question: How do you eat an elephant? *One bite at a time*. The more potential we have in terms of solving the problems we meet in life, the happier we are bound to be. Creativity itself cannot guarantee you happiness; but it can certainly be a great help.

In social matters, the ability to look creatively for alternatives is important if you are to enjoy being with others. Creativity enables you to look for ways of moving closer to another person. By thinking creatively about what you can do with another person that is active and enjoyable your life is made more exciting. This outlook and attitude is natural to some people but must be developed by others.

The creative process is more likely to occur when we expand our consciousness and mental processes. One thing that constricts thinking and creativity is criticism. Negative value judgments made by other people around us as we say or do things kill the incentive to be creative. We become afraid to try anything new. People impose limitations on themselves. They, in fact, have been conditioned to think they are unable to think creatively.

There are some basic rules to follow if you are to successfully apply creative thinking to solving your everyday problems. First, suspend all judgments and criticisms about the ideas you or anyone else come up with. This in itself frees the mind and enables you and everyone involved to think more freely and creatively. Begin by saying an idea that comes into your head about how to solve a particular problem. For instance, if the problem is boredom and you think there is nothing to do, you begin by stating whatever idea comes to mind. Each idea is potentially something you could do. If this is to work, you have to be openminded. No one should react by saying anything like, "That's dumb," or, "It'll never work." Just keep throwing out ideas one after another until you have developed a range of options. You might be tempted to set up a few criteria before you start out. Usually it is better if these are considered after the ideas have been developed. If you have to keep criteria in mind, the whole creative process is impaired. First develop the options, then the criteria. For example, if you have only five dollars to spend, don't limit your creative ideas or suggestions to five dollars. Often an expensive idea will lead to an inexpensive one. After the list is made, judge options according to the criteria you establish.

Keep on a "free-wheeling" basis. Keep the ideas coming, no matter how bizarre. Don't be afraid of getting a list that is too big. It is much easier to whittle down the list later than to try to add to it. And as one person offers an idea, it might trigger an even better idea from someone else who otherwise might not have had that idea. It is fun to bounce ideas off each other and to build on each other's ideas. The ideas get better and better as each person becomes more creative in his thought processes. Creativity encourages more creativity. Working on solutions to common problems together brings people closer. You feel good.

Remember to write down the ideas as they are being suggested. Writing them down preserves the thought so you can review them more thoroughly later. The more people you have involved in suggesting ideas, the better. The ideas then come fast and furious. You cannot remember them all, so have one or two people write them down.

Brainstorming by yourself is better than not doing it at all, but it is much better to have at least two or three people involved. The more the merrier. You get more ideas when you have more people.

Really make use of your mind in thinking creatively. You can solve problems you once thought were impossible. Scientists say that a person uses only a small fraction of his potential brainpower. If you learn to rely less on feelings and more on your thinking processes to overcome problems, you will be amazed at the positive things that will begin to happen in your life.

If you are lonely, try writing down one idea every day about what you can do specifically to over come loneliness. These are ideas that you can act on, regardless of how you feel or what another person does. Think of things you can do for or with others. After several weeks of jotting down these ideas, you will have a real "idea bank" full of ways you can enjoy life and get closer to another person. Choose one of the ideas and act on it.

Maybe you could keep some of these ideas in an envelope, put away for a rainy day when for some reason your creativity is not what it should be. Then you could draw on your idea bank for help. You can use this same process for ideas about things to do when you get bored or lonely. You will be surprised at how much it can help. Creative thinking can do wonders, if only you let it.

A young client, John, had become heavily involved with a girl and with drugs during his second year at college. After a while, his girl left him and moved in with his "best friend." He quit school, came home, went to his room, and stayed there for several weeks. At his parent's insistence, he came to see me.

Over a period of months, he got a job, returned to college and made a number of good friends. When we met the other night at a restaurant, his date commented on how different John had become.

"What is the biggest change you have seen in him?" I asked.

She thought for a minute and said, "He is always so full of ideas, of places to go and things to do. It is so much fun being with him." Then she added. "A year ago when I met him on a date over Christmas holidays, all he wanted to do was sit and drink beer and listen to music. He never wanted to do anything. Now I can't hold him down. He's really changed."

The creative thinking process helped John to see how good life could be if he were to open his mind to new ideas. A couple who had been fighting were referred for counseling by their family physcian. They both had recently been laid off at work. She started the conversation by saying she was so bored that her nerves were getting the best of her. "We can't do anything without money," she said. I took out a sheet of paper and a pencil; we started to make a list of things to do. As all three of us began throwing out ideas, they began to smile and get a little excited. Before we stopped, we had thirty-two possibilities, ten of them under two dollars. "I never thought it could be done," she said. And that is why she had not thought of it; she limited herself with a negative mind-set.

Both of these cases show how anyone can change his life with a little creative thinking. Living creatively means you listen, speak, observe, absorb life, and look for exciting things to do. Touch, see, hear, smell, taste, and live creatively. Then you will enjoy more of what life has to offer. You will be able to handle frustration, anxiety, and loneliness.

In coping with frustration, creative thinking is a big help. Try these steps the next time you get frustrated.

First, look at all the facts about your frustration. The specifics about what you are presently doing are important.

Second, ask the question you want answered. This is essential. You solve problems one at a time by zeroing in on them and bringing all your brainpower to bear on that precise problem.

Third, brainstorm ideas and come up with tentative solutions. You match these against the criteria and select a solution.

Fourth, before you attempt to implement your plan, again review the problem to see if it is worth the effort. Sometimes you might be better off to accept things the way they are. But once your mind is made up, go after your goal.

No one has a monopoly on brainpower and thinking. Sharing ideas and learning from others is one of life's greatest joys. Often others can help you to see more objectively what is happening in your life. You are the final judge of what is good or bad in your life, but others can help by giving you different ideas. Thinking is not necessarily hard work. It can really be fun. People think all the time. Some of us are faster than others and some better than others, but the tortoise has been known to beat the hare.

Don't ever sell yourself short. You can change if you make realistic plans and work at them. The paradox of happiness is that you first must give in order to get. Steer clear of negative people who are always critical of everything life has to offer. Use your time and your talents wisely, but use them.

Man, now more than ever, must utilize his thinking ability to live more creatively if he is to overcome loneliness. Being able genuinely to enjoy life and to feel happier and healthier are goals you can achieve. Self-improvement or a change in the way you live is possible if you do not concentrate on your problems and on what happened in the past. Concentrate on positive solutions and doing worthwhile things which involve you with others. Preoccupation with problems can be replaced with friends and involvement.

Instead of self-defeat and gloom, you can become the cause of good events in your life. You do not have to be the victim of your own poor choices. Creative thinking can make your life come alive. Loneliness, boredom, broken relationships, and feelings of failure need no longer be a part of your life. The choice is yours.

A good friend of mine recently lost her husband. She had been sitting at home, moaning and crying. "How does staying at home help you?" I asked. "Does it make you happier?"

"No," she said, "but I'm so miserable." The bad feelings caused by the death of her husband grew increasingly worse each day she stayed at home. Ultimately she chose to go back to work. Once at work, she began to re-enter the world of people she had temporarily left. She had caused herself to feel better by changing what she was doing.

Each of us decides the quality of our own lives. Look at your life and decide what you want to do with it now. Never be satisfied with what happened yesterday. Use your abilities to grow and keep growing. With all your great potential, why be lonely?

Those interested in Reality Therapy
are invited to contact:

William Glasser, M.D.
Institute for Reality Therapy
11633 San Vicente Boulevard
Los Angeles, CA 90049

Edward E. Ford, M.S.S.A.
Regional Associate
Institute for Reality Therapy
3808 Belmont Avenue
Youngstown, OH 44505